Discourse of Blogs and Wikis

Continuum Discourse Series

Series Editor: Professor Ken Hyland, Institute of Education, University of London.

Discourse is one of the most significant concepts of contemporary thinking in the humanities and social sciences as it concerns the ways language mediates and shapes our interactions with each other and with the social, political and cultural formations of our society. The *Continuum Discourse Series* aims to capture the fast-developing interest in discourse to provide students, new and experienced teachers and researchers in applied linguistics, ELT and English language with an essential bookshelf. Each book deals with a core topic in discourse studies to give an in-depth, structured and readable introduction to an aspect of the way language is used in real life.

Other titles in the series:

Academic Discourse
Ken Hyland

Metadiscourse: Exploring Interaction in Writing
Ken Hyland

Using Corpora in Discourse Analysis
Paul Baker

Discourse Analysis: An Introduction
Brian Paltridge

Media Discourse
Joanna Thornborrow

School Discourse: Learning to Write across the Years of Schooling
Frances Christie and Beverly Derewianka

Professional Discourse
Britt-Louise Gunnarsson

Discourse of Blogs and Wikis

Greg Myers

continuum

Continuum International Publishing Group

The Tower Building
11 York Road
London SE1 7NX

80 Maiden Lane
Suite 704
New York, NY 10038

British Library Cataloguing-in-Publication Data
A catalogue record for this book is available from the British Library.

ISBN: 978-1-8470-6413-4 (hardback)
         978-1-8470-6414-1 (paperback)

Library of Congress Cataloging-in-Publication Data
Myers, Greg, 1954-
Blog and wiki discourse / Greg Myers.
    p. cm.
Includes bibliographical references and index.
ISBN 978-1-84706-413-4
1. Language and the Internet. 2. Communication and technology.
3. Discourse analysis. 4. Blogs. 5. Wikis (Computer science) I. Title.

P96.L34.M94 2009
401´.41–dc22

2009034844

Typeset by Newgen Imaging Systems Pvt Ltd, Chennai, India
Printed and bound in Great Britain by CPI Antony Rowe, Chippenham, Wiltshire

for Tess

Contents

Preface

There are two reasons to write about the language of blogs and wikis:

1. The innovations in these rapidly developing genres can help us focus on aspects of language we might take for granted in more stable genres such as newspapers and sonnets.
2. A focus on details of language use may help us see aspects of what bloggers and Wikipedians do that may be missed by analysts focusing more on the technology.

There are many aspects of the language that could be studied, including grammar, spelling and innovative lexis. I have focused on discourse, that is the language as a social practice, the way it is used in interactions between people. That is why I have chapters on links, place, time and collaboration, topics that you might not think would be central in a book on language.

Here are a few suggestions about using the book. I have intended chapters to be read through, so I have generally kept methodological details and references until the end of each chapter. There is not yet a large literature on the language of blogs and wikis, though as you will see, there are some excellent early academic studies that I have tried to follow. Most of my references are to studies of language use more generally, usually textbooks and introductory texts, so that readers can follow up in much more detail the analytical issues that I have just suggested. I thought that full references to the permanent link for every short quotation would be too distracting, so I have just given the URLs at the end of the book for all the blogs used, along with the dates sampled so that you can find them in the blog archives.

I have tried to be consistent in my use of format conventions. *Italics* are used for names of blogs, for stress, and for mentioning rather than using the words themselves (*now* means I am talking about that word, not using it to refer to the present moment). <u>Underlines</u> are retained in blog quotations to indicate links. **Bold** is added in examples to indicate the feature I am discussing; it was not put there by the blogger. ***Bold italics*** indicate a word that has an entry in the Glossary. I have kept the exact spelling of each quotation from a blog, not using *sic* to indicate unconventional spelling or usage; the unconventionality can be (though it is not always) part of the style of the blogger.

I have accumulated many debts in the course of writing this book. It began as advice to students on the BA English Language and the Media at Lancaster, and I have learned a lot from their projects. I first thought of it as a possible book when there was an invitation from Santiago Posteguillo and Inmaculada Fortanet to give a talk while I was at Universitat Jaume I in Castelló, Spain; I offered them a list of topics of lectures from my courses and research, and they leapt at this one (or leapt away from the other possibilities). There were further talks at the British Association for Applied Linguistics in Edinburgh, an Arts and Humanities Research Council workshop at the Open University (my thanks to Theresa Lillis), AELFE at Madrid (Maria Kuteeva), a departmental lecture at the Centre for Research in Linguistics and Language Sciences at the University of Newcastle (Christopher Jenks), a conference on the Knowledge Society at Lancaster and a short inaugural lecture at the Lancaster Ideas Festival. And I am grateful to Gurdeep Mattu and Colleen Coulter at Continuum, and to Ken Hyland for finding a home for this title in his series on Discourse.

I have tried to contact all the bloggers I studied, in case they preferred not to have their words excerpted this way. My thanks to those who responded; all of them gave permission.

My colleagues Ruth Wodak, David Barton and Julia Gillen have inspired and challenged parts of this, directly or indirectly, and I benefitted from comments from Julia, David, Jane Sunderland, Jane Mulderrig, Johnny Unger, Veronika Koller, Mick Short, Anne Cronin, Bronislaw Szerszynski, Mick Short and Jonathan Culpeper. Tess Cosslett not only gave comments, she put up with this project over two years in which I kept quoting clever bits I had found on blogs that day, or yet another strange bit of *Wikipedia*.

1 Introduction: A linguist in the blogosphere

The chapter in a sentence: New kinds of interaction such as blogs and wikis can provide good materials for the study of language in use, and raise issues for the study of other kinds of texts.

1.1 Why study blogs and wikis?

It is the evening of 21 June 2006, the summer solstice, and I am on British Summer Time, at Latitude 54° 3' North, Longitude 2° 48.2' West. Here is a quick tour of some blogs on my Favourites list:

- *Boing Boing* (www.boingboing.net) links me to the Earth Science Picture of the Day, with over a million starlings.
- *Litrate News* (http://litrate.blogspot.com/) has a picture of a bus driver on the motorway reading, or, as these literacy researchers put it, 'Driver supports literacy programme'.
- Heidi Swanson at *101 Cookbooks* (http://101cookbooks.com) has found some home-made collage and comic cookbooks on the Flickr site (I like the crude cartoon version with very bad advice on cooking pasta).
- Jonathan Edelstein at *HeadHeeb* (http://headheeb.blogmosis. com/) has a long and thoughtful discussion, with many links, in response to an Israeli cabinet decision to liberalize naturalization criteria, leading to the wider issue, 'can the Jewish people be separated from the religion of Judaism'?
- Glenn Reynolds at *Instapundit* (http://www.instapundit.com) has a quotation from another blog on a report on affirmative action and Asian Pacific applicants: 'THIS SEEMS PRETTY DAMNING where college admissions are concerned'.
- Amit Varma at *India Uncut* (http://indiauncut.blogspot.com/) has an entry entitled 'Rashomon', 'Did they elope or was she abducted?' (the links lead to two contrasting news stories).
- Sean at *Cosmic Variance* (http://cosmicvariance.com) links to three bloggers pointing out sexism in scientific institutions (such as addressing male post-docs as 'Dr' while calling female post-docs by their first names).

I could go on, but then this book wouldn't get written. There is something addictive about blogs, reading on one's lunch-hour, or before getting down to some work in the evening, following a link and then another link. I am told there is something addictive about writing them too, though my own blogging has been rather erratic.

In Chapter 2 I deal in some detail with the question of what blogs and wikis are. For now we can start with Rebecca Blood's definition of *blog*: 'a frequently updated webpage with dated entries, new ones placed on top' (Blood 2002a: 12; Blood 2002c: vi) and the definition of *wiki* in *Wikipedia*: 'a page or collection of Web pages designed to enable anyone who accesses it to contribute or modify content, using a simplified markup language.' Blogs are not like personal home pages, because they are regularly updated, and they are not like diaries, because they are built around links, and they are not like wikis, which involve many authors collaborating on one text. They usually have links to other sites on the web, and comments on those links, and may have a list of other blogs that might interest the reader of this one. They can contain text, pictures, sounds and video. None of this suggests the enormous range of uses to which they are put, and the discussion they have generated, since weblog sites first became popular in 1999. They are changing very rapidly now, and even the simplest figures and lists of popular blogs become outdated in months. I just came across a blog that regularly provides new mp3 sound files of cats purring – surely not an application originally envisioned by the developers of the software.

To those not (yet) involved with blogs, they may seem just another internet fad, something sent to you in a link from one of your more technically literate friends, like webcams of the surf at La Jolla, sites reuniting schoolmates, a video clip of buffalos fighting lions, or Google Earth. But after years of being about to be really big, blogs now really *are* very big. Newspapers seriously discuss the influence of bloggers on the selection of the last US Democratic Presidential candidate; newspaper and broadcast journalists have their own blogs; and many of the best blogs lead to book publication. Last year the Edinburgh Fringe Festival had no less than three plays based on blogs (this year it was *Facebook* – you've got to keep up). And they are now regularly the topic of academic conference papers and PhD dissertations (see 'What I read').

The best known wiki application, *Wikipedia*, has flourished in the same time period as blogs, and has also had a huge amount of media attention, and like blogs, it is the result of a relatively small technological innovation that has led to radically different uses. Like blogs, it has received both dismissive and hyperbolic coverage in traditional media. But for the analysis I am doing here, wikis are the opposite of blogs:

where wikis are impersonal by definition, blogs are often personal in their style and point of view, and where wikis strive to achieve a consensus on a single page, presented for the moment as definitive, the blogosphere delights in diversity and conflict, even in one post. A wiki is a device for putting people together, and a blog is a device for setting them apart as individuals.

You could read the huge amounts of writing that bloggers and wikipedians (who are neither shy nor unreflexive) pour out about themselves and the forms they have developed, on the web and in books. And you could read the stories in almost any magazine that deals with business, technology or popular culture (see 'What I read'). Why devote academic study to these texts?

- First, if blogs are becoming important in political, social and economic life, we need to know how they work, just as we need to know about political speeches, journalism and advertisements. The persuaded have to know what the persuaders are doing.
- Second, looking at a medium as it emerges helps us think better about other media that we take for granted. So we might notice the linguistic conventions they use for locating themselves, dealing with others and stating facts and opinions, just because blogs as a genre are emerging, unstable, changing from month to month. The same sort of elaborate rhetorical moves in newspapers or academic articles may seem unremarkable because they are familiar.
- Third, blogs really use the web. There have been lots of linguistic studies of the web (see 'What I read'), but many of the pages studied are just like print ads or corporate reports or newspapers. Blogs use the links, the international reach, the search engines, the capacity for including various kinds of material, visual and verbal and aural. They are, as Rebecca Blood says, 'native to the web'.
- And the same issues apply to wikis. If students and others are going to use *Wikipedia* as a form of reference (often going against the advice or guidelines of their teachers), then they also need to be able to read it critically. Even if one doesn't use *Wikipedia*, one needs to be able to think about how it could potentially transform our ways of producing consensus knowledge. And wikis are another innovation that uses the web as a platform so that the combined resources of tens of thousands of people can be brought to bear on one project, a project that was possible but was not even imagined 10 years ago.

3

And why focus on *language* in the blogs and wikis? There are lots of studies of other aspects, especially those most easily quantified. And there is a tendency in studies of new media to play up the visual and aural elements and to treat writing as, well, old. But despite all the possibilities open to bloggers for inclusion of pictures, sound and video, written language remains central to most blogs. At some of the most popular blogs the main attraction is the inventive, personal and highly compressed writing, not any urgent information (The style of *Wikipedia* is less fun, for reasons I will go into in Chapter 9). By studying language, we can take a step back (or perhaps a step closer) and look intensely at how they say things, as well as what they say. This turns out to be a useful move with blogs, as it is with other kinds of written texts. Also, blogs and wikis lead out from linguistic issues to wider issues about the use of language in society. Among these issues are the ways we use language to locate ourselves, to state facts, to argue and to define ourselves in relation to other people. Bloggers and Wikipedians sometimes seem to have everything they want, with free software, lots of neat add-ons, all the resources of the web at their disposal, and a host of gurus, consultants and commentators. But what they really need, I think, is a linguist poring over their words.

When I say I am analyzing language, I do not just mean picking out the aspects of language that most interest the press, the invention of neologisms (such as 'blog' itself), and acronyms (such as 'WTF' or 'MSM'), and their playful use (for instance, a noun becoming a verb). I mean the exploitation of a range of linguistic features, from the more obvious to the less obvious: pronouns and deixis, address forms and sentence types, implicatures and politeness, stance and evidentials and hedges (don't worry, I explain all these terms later, or see the Glossary). Many of the tools developed for analysing advertising, political speeches, newspaper articles, academic articles or essays work well on blogs (and some don't work, but fail in interesting ways – I found less hedging and less deixis than I expected).

I can already hear some objections: that blogs are too trivial in content ('my cat did something cute'), too diverse (see the list at the beginning of the chapter), too ephemeral (everything can look different a day later), and maybe too much like existing, already heavily analysed media (websites, alternative journalism, ads) to be worth intensive analysis. All possibly true. But each of these objections is, I think, good enough reason to write a book about blogs and wikis. Blogs are by no means always about trivial topics, but the best of them remain engaged with the everyday, even when they are about the US Constitution, Digital Rights Management on music CDs, financial derivatives or gamma ray emissions from the moon. Blogs deal with diverse topics, but I will argue

4

that some similarities are emerging between most members of the genre, because routines emerge as people do the same kinds of social acts again and again. Blogs are ephemeral, but that is good enough reason to try to take a snapshot as they flash by, and look closely at it. Blogs are like lots of other media – diaries, newspapers, magazines, photo albums, discussion lists, cookbooks – drawing on them, adapting them, parodying them, and for that reason they can tell us about those other media, even as they lead us into a new medium we don't yet quite understand.

Similar complaints are made about *Wikipedia*: critics like to show how some 'trivial' topic gets more space than some 'important' topic, it provides breadth rather than detail, it leaves errors uncorrected, it is constantly changing, and it is just a second-rate free encyclopaedia. And similar responses can be made. *Wikipedia* at its best makes knowledge accessible in a way that academic specialists aren't always able or willing to do, it covers topics that aren't considered worthy of attention, it keeps up (while even the best expert encyclopaedia is out of date as soon as it is published). And it might be argued, despite its name, that *Wikipedia* isn't much like a print encyclopaedia at all, but is more like other kinds of collaborative projects based on the web as a platform, such as open source software.

I am interested in those aspects of blog and wiki language that can tell us what people are doing with them: how they use blogs and wikis in social interaction, and how blogs and wikis have emerged as a distinctive kind of text and as a distinctive way of reporting, commenting, arguing and making sense. I'm especially interested in these issues:

- When you come across a blog on the web, how do you know what it is and how it works (Chapter 2)?
- How do blogs hold together when they consist largely of links to other texts (Chapter 3)?
- How do blogs and bloggers situate themselves in the geographical world and in the blogosphere, using deixis, adverbials, narratives and other linguistic devices (Chapter 4)?
- How do these date-stamped texts, apparently stuck in the moment of the date stamp, construct time (Chapter 5)?
- How do blogs and bloggers project audiences (Chapter 6)?
- How do blogs and bloggers construct their opinions (Chapter 7)?
- How do blogs and bloggers support and modify statements of fact (Chapter 8)?
- How do Wikipedians collaborate on a text (Chapter 9)?
- How do Wikipedians handle disagreements about the text (Chapter 10)?

5

1.2 Example

Let's take an hour and a half of postings from the popular US political blog *Instapundit* on Saturday, 24 June 2006.

THE NOTE:

The Democrats' Iraq policy is NOT 'cut and run' (Reed and Kerry), NOT 'irresponsible' or 'unpatriotic' (Reid), and NOT based on 'political considerations,' (Feingold).
Glad that's cleared up.

posted at 01:04 PM by Glenn Reynolds

EGYPTIAN BLOGGER ALAA has been released from prison.

posted at 11:30 AM by Glenn Reynolds

SO THE BEACH HOUSE WE RENTED came with this cool deck chair, which everybody loved. I liked it so much that I wrote down the name, searched it on the Web, and ordered one from Amazon. It reclines kind of like one of those zero-gravity recliner chairs, and even though it folds up neatly for storage, it's not rickety like most folding deck chairs. Downside – it's not especially cheap. But given my unsatisfactory experiences with its predecessors, I'm happy.

Perhaps it will encourage me to spend more time on the deck drinking beer, and less time at the computer . . . .

posted at 11:27 AM by Glenn Reynolds ✇

1.3 Genre

Let's say you came across this page, not because you were a regular reader of *Instapundit*, but because you happened to type 'deck chair' and 'beer' into Google (and if you did that just after the post, this item would have been on top of the list, because *Instapundit* is a very popular site). How would you know you were looking at a blog? Well to begin with, it *looks* like a blog: (you can see it at http://www.pajamas-media.com/instapundit/archives/week_2006_06_18.php).

The main part of this page is taken up with a scroll of short items, each giving the name of the person who posted it (always Glenn Reynolds, in this case) and time of posting. Every once in a while, there is a heading for a new date. Each item also has some text in blue, which turns out to be a link to the source of the story on which he is commenting (As we will see in Chapter 3, not all blogs are based on links like this, but many are). This list is in reverse chronological order; if I check the page a few hours later (this is a very prolific blogger), there will be more items on the page, and this one will be pushed further down the long scroll, until it is finally pushed off into the archives. The 'About' link in the upper left tells us that Reynolds is a Professor of Law at the University of Tennessee. There are ads on the right for Professor Reynolds' podcasts, his book, other books and blogs, and Pajamas Media, a commercial site to which he is one of the best known contributors. Further down is his blogroll, lists of other blogs he finds interesting (so we see, for instance, that he lists mainly conservative and libertarian political blogs – not a place to find either Democrats or cake recipes). All these features are common to many blogs. There is also the visual design of the blog – simple but distinctive enough that it can be sent up by a parodist.

So what is this – a personal web page, a directory, a diary, a political pamphlet? Does a blog have to have links? Dates? One author? I will explore these issues in Chapter 2. My broader concern there is how a technical innovation – the software that allows easy posting to a web page without knowing HTML, such as Pyra's first Blogger – shapes and is shaped by what people want to do with it. The software certainly does not determine the content, as shown by the unpredictable and bizarre array of blogs out there, but it does provide some opportunities, for instance making it easier to post links with comments, and to update pages.

1.4 Texts and intertextuality

When I have studied texts before in my academic career, it was usually pretty clear what the text was. An ad was a page of a magazine that looked quite different from the editorial content, a poem had a title and then a number of lines until a white space at end, and a scientific article started with the title and names and institutions of authors, and ended with acknowledgements and references. It seemed reasonable to take all the words between the beginning and the ending, and maybe categorize them and count them; the text was one coherent unit. The example I have offered here is more and less than a coherent unit. It is more than a unit in that it is made up of three separate postings, on the same day, by the same person, but not necessarily related in content (war policy, human rights, deck chairs), style or purpose. What I have quoted is clearly just an excerpt from a larger text, but this text keeps getting bigger, as long as Professor Reynolds is awake. Like a television soap opera, a blog is open-ended by definition, and is dead when it stops adding new chapters. My sample is less than a unit in that each of these texts is built around another text that may be quoted here (as in the posting from 'The Note') or may just be a link (as in the report about Alaa). Are these linked texts part of this text, or do they only enter it when quoted?

Discourse analysts and literary critics have been trying for decades to break up the idea of the single unified text, with a single author, and have paid more attention to intertextuality, the way one text draws on and responds to others. This can sometimes seem a rather specialized practice (as with a poem alluding to the work of an earlier poet) or an abstract notion, when all discourse is seen as a sort of dialogue in which speakers or writers respond to and anticipate other words. Blogs started from weblogs, lists of links to interesting sites on the web, so the intertextuality is not something that comes later or is attributed by analysts – it was there at the beginning. And the intertextuality is not some secret code to be guessed at by aficionados (as with allusions to film noir in current movies); it is clearly marked (in this case, by blue ink and underlining). There has been a great deal of academic comment on hypertext, partly because it fits so neatly with current theories of literature and discourse; in Chapter 3 I will discuss the different forms of these links, and their uses. The best blogs use links in a witty way, so that one only sees the full meaning by following the link. And just as academics write their articles to get cited, bloggers post their entries in the hopes that other bloggers will link to them (handbooks include various tricks for making this more likely). Such links can have dramatic consequences; a previously unvisited site that is linked to by the highly popular *Instapundit* can find its server crashing under the weight of thousands of hits, a phenomenon referred to, apparently, as an 'Instalanche'.

1.5 Locating blogs

Our sense of space and time are tied to language, with pointing words such as *here* and *there*, *then* and *now*, and other expressions that have their meaning based on the location of the speaker and hearer. It has often been pointed out that the internet (and other electronic media) destabilize this sense, by stretching another grid of places and times over the coordinates we get from maps and clocks. 'Here' in a blog typically refers not to the place where the author is writing (such as Tennessee) or even the text as a place ('Here at *Instapundit*'), but is more typically a gesture to another place, a link to another text. Many attempts have been made to map the abstract space that is constructed by all these links, to show, for instance, the tight cluster of links around *Instapundit* in relation to the distinct cluster around the US liberal political blog *The Daily Kos*.

When we look closer at the texts of blogs, we see the default, taken for granted location is a kind of placelessness: neutral, unmeaning, an overview. The spatial default is a time-stamp (which as we have seen, comes with every post) that suggests clock time unreeling in a uniform and universal way. Within this vision, that is both utopian and a bit scary, bloggers use space and time references for specific purposes. They construct meaningful places and narratives, sometimes with the slightest and most indirect forms of self-location. These switches have specific effects: contrasting, justifying, evaluating or evoking the physical body of the blogger. So the blogosphere is not quite so radically different a spatial (see Chapter 4) and temporal (see Chapter 5) world as one might think from the claims sometimes made for it.

1.6 Audience

One of the clichés of media studies over the last 30 years has been that audiences are not passive recipients of messages, but active participants in shaping media texts and using media in their own practices. This usually takes some explaining when one is talking about a popular magazine or television programme. But with blogs, the audience is always at least potentially there in the text: suggesting links to the author, making links to the blog entry (which may then show up on the page as trackbacks), and in some cases posting comments in the blog itself. All these functions are easily set up in blog software, and one can see them, for instance, in *BoingBoing*.

The example from *Instapundit* that I have used has none of these devices in its posts. Reynolds does often include comments, corrections and links from readers. But the textual indications of audience here are more implicit. Since I am not in the US, and don't follow the kinds of scandals and accusations that interest right-wing American commentators, *Instapundit* items are often incomprehensible to me, even when I follow the links. For instance, to make sense of the first posting, it helps to know that *The Note* is a political commentary on the ABC website, and to know enough about US politics of the moment to recognize these surnames of Democrats (without any given names), and more broadly, to recognize the clichés of the debates about Iraq war policy. Reynolds' comment, 'Glad that's cleared up' projects an ironic stance; that it needs no further comment projects an audience that shares his view that the Democrats' policy is properly described by the kinds of terms rejected here. The second post makes a simpler statement of a news item; it is characteristic of the kind of quick annotation Reynolds favours. That Alaa Seif al-Islam is identified as 'Egyptian blogger' suggests we may not have heard of his case; the link then tells us more. The third item suggests an audience in a different way, using a conversational formula 'So . . .' to introduce a narrative. And the closing joke draws on our awareness as readers that Professor Reynolds demonstrably spends a lot of time in front of the computer, since postings appear throughout the day. In Chapter 6, I consider the ways blogs project audiences and enact interaction with them.

1.7 Opinions

Blogs have been greeted with joy or despair as outlets for the unbridled expression of opinion: comments, suggestions, reviews, outcries, rants. Almost all other outlets for such expressions are controlled in some way: one has to be hired to write a column in a newspaper or make a speech at a conference, and even letters to the editor are heavily selected and edited. Callers to radio phone-ins don't often get through, or get the time to say what they want, and bumper stickers can't really carry much text. Not all of us can express our opinions by giving millions to political campaigns. But anyone with internet access can blog. I don't need to know anything about jazz, the Congress, Iraq, vaccines, Finland, or pasta to express an opinion in the strongest terms, to anyone who will bother to read it. That's one reason that blogs are in general rather boring, and very occasionally fascinating.

When blogs began their sudden rise to prominence in 1999, users of bulletin boards and discussion lists had already had a great deal of experience with the etiquette of argument on the web. Everyone knew that these personal but anonymous contacts could lead to emotionally hurtful and intellectually unhelpful rages, and that rumours and hoaxes could circulate rapidly. Bloggers do not necessarily follow any traditional forms of argumentation, but they have developed some practices of persuasion that, when they work, allow people to keep on writing and interacting, even when the world is full of idiots. I consider some of the emerging conventions of persuasion in Chapter 7.

1.8 Facts

Blogs take up some of the functions of newspapers and other traditional ways of getting information, but with a more personal perspective and less institutional weight (see Gillmor 2004; Allan 2006). So we might expect to find a lot of statements of fact, and some marking of the writer's stance on these statements, for instance modal verbs and mental process verbs (e.g., *I think*), the kinds of linguistic devices that have been grouped together under the heading of *evidentiality*. But the one statement of fact in the example comes unhedged: 'Egyptian blogger Alaa has been released from prison'. It is not 'may have been released' or 'it is claimed that he was released' or 'I think he has been released'. I have been surprised to find how rarely bloggers state facts, unless they are (like *Baghdad Burning*) essentially doing first-hand reporting. It may be that (there I go, hedging) statements can be made without the explicit marking of stance because they are supported by links – someone else is making the claim.

I argue in Chapter 8 that statements of fact are measured less against any scale of evidentiality and more against shared expectations. A statement is interesting when it confirms those expectations (for Reynolds and his readers, the hypocrisy of Democrats), links to what is already known (the blogger who was in jail is now out), or defies expectations (the chair is not rickety, and not cheap). I can see the linguistic markers of expectation even more clearly in some of the more technical blogs, for instance on astrophysics or net neutrality regulations, because there I am party to none of the expectations that might reasonably be supposed for a competent reader. The reader of blogs is not just picking up bits and pieces of information; he or she is constantly testing out membership in a group, perhaps a very small group, of people who know the kind of thing the blogger is writing about.

1.9 Wikis and blogs

I take up wikis at the end of the book because I think they help us understand blogs, by contrast. Both are based on software innovations that enable users to deal with the vast proliferation of material on the web. The blog solution is to have each blogger 'publish, then filter'

(Shirky 2008: Ch. 4); readers have to sort out the good stuff from the bad by relying on their judgement, popularity and comments of other bloggers. The wiki solution is to have a page that can be edited by any-one to add or remove information, change the style, or update material. To keep this process from leading to chaos, *Wikipedia* has a set of guiding principles on what can be said and on how disputes are to be resolved. Other wikis, such as *Citizendium*, have modified these principles, but the idea remains the same: one needs to have a lot of people working on the page for it to work, and one needs some explicitly stated rules of interaction.

One reads *Instapundit* to get Glenn Reynolds' distinctive take on material he has found on the internet. In contrast, one might look up an article on *Wikipedia* to find out who Glenn Reynolds is. There one will, indeed, find a page giving some biographical information and refer-ences to his publications, with a picture. As I explain in Chapter 2, the important feature of the page is that anyone can edit it, and discuss their changes. Here is part of the 'Talk' page on 'Glenn Reynolds':

> Who said 'conservative' was pejorative? I only removed it because it was inaccurate – you stated that you 'inferred' he is a conserva-tive, from what I don't know. Reynolds is pro-choice and supports gay rights, and has frequently described himself as having libertar-ian beliefs. I disagree that Reynolds is a POV source when it comes to his own political orientation, as long as it is stated in the right way. 'Reynolds describes himself as a libertarian' would be an accurate, NPOV way of presenting that. Inserting the adjective 'con-servative' is not only inaccurate, it is <u>original research</u>, since you 'inferred' that he is a conservative and that he runs a 'distinctly non-liberal' blog. The reason I simply removed 'conservative' rather than replacing it with 'libertarian' is that I wanted to find a post on his blog in which he self-describes as a libertarian before making that assertion, so we would have <u>verifiable</u> information in the article.

I won't try to settle this dispute between *Ben Houston* and *Android 79*. What interests me is the way both sides refer to Wikipedia Principles, such as Neutral Point of View (NPOV), No Original Research (NOR) and Verifiability. There are also special rules for BLPs – Biographies of Living Persons (a category which would, of course, include Professor Reynolds). At first glance, these principles may seem naïve – after all, we know there can be no neutral point of view (as this exchange shows). But in practice, they are not so simple; they are not statements about the production of new knowledge (which is explicitly excluded from Wikipedia), but about ways of presenting specialist knowledge to a gen-eral reader. They enable participants to refer to some shared presumably shared aims, and they are constantly tested out on a series of cases, backed by more discussion and a kind of emerging case law. To my surprise, these processes work rather well; *Wikipedia* articles may have errors in them, but they typically get better over time. Examination of some of these discussions will enable us to reflect on some of the issues in the book: the definition of a genre, intertextuality, time, facts and rhetoric.

1.10 So what?

I hope that close analysis of this sort can help us understand discourse more generally. I also think it can contribute to discussions of the big social issues around blogs and wikis. Why is there such a huge difference in readership between a few hugely popular blogs and the millions of blogs with what have been called 'nano-audiences'? How does information, rumour, or a witty remark circulate so quickly? How do clusters of bloggers form and maintain themselves? How does the collective authority of the blogosphere relate to the traditional authority of professional journalists, doctors, lawyers or teachers? How does the collective authority of *Wikipedia* relate to the traditional authority of academic experts? These kinds of questions need political scientists to look at opinion formation, sociologists to look at identities, systems researchers to look at networks, and user studies to look at software. But they also need a linguist.

1.11 What I read

Rather than break up the text with lists of general references, I will group them at the end of each chapter (I will still give references in the text for specific quotations and terms). I hope this will make it easier for readers to collect the rather scattered sources for each chapter.

In my view, the best collection on blogs so far is Bruns and Jacobs (2006), and as my references show, I've found a lot of useful suggestions in a Bruns' more recent book (2008) and in a non-academic but thoughtful book by Clay Shirky (2008). Rebecca Blood's definition of 'blog' and her remark about their use of the web are to be found in *We've Got Blog* (Rodzvilla 2002); she also had a number of papers linked to her blog, listed below, and a handbook (Blood 2002b), which is more of a practical start-up guide than a commentary. *We've Got Blog* reprints notes by early figures in the development of blogs, there is also a collection of essays and interviews by Kline and Burstein (2005), and there are a number of anecdotal collections such as that by right-wing journalist and blogger Hugh Hewitt (2005). For an academic overview of the organization of the blogosphere, see Kumar, Novak, Raghavan and Tomkins (2004). Gillmor's (2004) and Allan's (2006) books on blog journalism manage to avoid the breathless tone of some of the more hype-filled collections of anecdotes.

I have not yet found any books on blog language, though Stephanie Nilsson has posted a paper that makes a useful starting point (2004), and Scott Nowson has an Edinburgh PhD focusing on differences in individual style (2006). On the language of the web more generally, see Crystal (2001) and Boardman (2005), both intended as introductions, and Posteguillo (2003), which offers more of a general framework. Susan Herring and her colleagues have a series of papers (Herring, Scheidt et al.; Herring, Kouper et al. 2005; Herring and Paolillo 2006), some of which will be discussed in the next chapter. There are useful papers taking a rhetorical approach in an online collection edited by Gurak, Antonijevic, Johnson, Ratliff and Reyman (2004).

2 Genre: What is a blog? What is a wiki?

The chapter in a sentence: Blogs and wikis are genres of texts defined not so much by their form or content as by the kinds of uses to which they are put, and the ways these uses construct social identities and communities.

Go to a computer, open a browser, enter this URL in the address box, and hit return:

> http://www.101cookbooks.com/archives/berry-beer-baked-beans-recipe.html

Now open a new window, and enter this address:

> http://en.wikipedia.org/wiki/Fun_Home

(Or if those URLs have shifted between the time I wrote this and you read it, you could just enter '101 cookbooks berry beer baked beans' and then 'Wikipedia Fun Home' in the Google search box; those are likely to be the first pages on the results list.) Now tell me what it is you see.

For the first page, you might once have said it was a recipe, or a letter addressed to the author's dad, or a web page with a lot of ads and links. But now you probably say it is a blog. For the second page, you might once have said it was an encyclopaedia article or a book review. But now you certainly recognize it as *Wikipedia*. What you have done is put the page you see into a genre, a type of text that you think will be recognized by the person you are talking to. **Genres** are types of texts that share certain features because their users share certain purposes. Usually these types have names: sonnets and limericks are genres of poems, westerns and musicals are genres of movies, mysteries and chicklit are genres in book publishing, news and phone-ins are genres of radio programmes and research articles and textbooks are genres of academic publication (*Fun Home*, the book that is the topic of the Wikipedia article is itself a hybrid of two genres, the memoir and the graphic novel). Texts in genres are similar to each other, and they are similar for a reason, because people want to do the same sorts of

15

things over and over again. For instance, students who miss seminars are supposed to send me a note (now usually an email), and these notes are similar in their forms of address, content and closing, even though students were never told just what they should include. They arrive at a form because the act of excusing an absence is something students do repeatedly – though I hope not too often.

I am going to ask a series of questions based on Carol Berkenkotter's and Tom Huckin's conceptualization of genre (1995). I will start where the genres come from (and where they are going), then consider what they look like, and then link this to the ways they fit into what people do with them, and into social networks and communities.

2.1 Where does this genre come from and where is it going?

The origins of some genres (the epic, the novel or the skipping rhyme) lead back into the mists of time. But both blogs and wikis have almost legendary stories of their beginnings, told and retold by their users, that lead us only as far back as 1995 (See Table 2.1). The two stories parallel each other chronologically.

Rebecca Blood (2002c) traces the origin of 'links with commentary, with the new stuff on top' to various website designers in 1997, Jorn Barger gave these the name *weblog* in 1998, and Peter Merholz said he

Table 2.1 Conventional histories of blogs and wikis, divided into stages

Stages	Blogs	Wikipedia
legendary founders of the concept – 1995–1999	Jorn Barger, Cameron Barrett, Peter Merholz – weblogs and we blog, 1998	Ward Cunningham and *WikiWikiWeb*, 1995
the application – 1999–2000	Pitas and Pyra software, 1999	*Wikipedia*, 2001
the explosion of interest – 2001–2004	by 2004, 4 million blogs, 12,000 new ones per day	by 2004, about 200,000 articles, more or less doubling each year
models available to the first users	home pages, diaries, newspaper columns	encyclopaedias
new tools	Technorati and other search sites, shared tags (as at del.icio.us) RSS feeds that automatically add content	bots that make automatic corrections, templates that force consistency between articles, watch lists
problems	spam, numbers of bloggers, commercialization	vandalism, trolls, edit wars, bureaucracy
challengers	*MySpace, Facebook, Twitter, Flickr*	*Citizendium, Conservapedia*

would treat it as *we blog*, giving birth to the term *blog*. In 1999, two small software companies, Pitas and Pyra, produced tools that made it easy for users unfamiliar with HTML coding to produce such sites from their browser. This software made blogging accessible beyond the community of systems designers and techies, with people using it for personal diaries, political commentaries, special interest groups, reports from the war, reviews, recipes, photos and all sorts of other uses. Users already knew what a regular newspaper column looked like, or a recipe, so they already had some genres in mind. But these genres changed subtly, or not so subtly, when they had links and commentators and the possibility of constant revision. In 2003, Google bought out Pyra's Blogger software; Google's site is still the largest base for blogs. Most of the most-widely read bloggers started in the years 2001–2005; there are still lots of people starting blogging every year (as the figures in Technorati's 'State of the Blogosphere' show), but it is no longer a Wild West in which any gunslinger fast on the draw could become a sheriff.

Ward Cunningham developed the wiki, a tool for collaborative editing of a web page, in a site called WikiWikiWeb, in 1995 (see 'Wiki' on Wikipedia). There have been many uses for this software, in online projects on travel or other issues, and in businesses. In 2001, Jimmy Wales and Larry Sanger founded *Wikipedia*, by far the best-known application of wikis, after earlier unsuccessful attempts to create an online encyclopaedia with paid expert contributors (see 'History of *Wikipedia*' in *Wikipedia,* and also Bruns (2008)). Clay Shirky points out the crucial importance of what is apparently a detail, the use of the '-pedia' suffix:

> Though wikis can be used for many kinds of writing, the early users were guided by the rhetorical models of existing encyclopedias, which helped synchronize the early work: there was a shared awareness of the kind of writing that should go into a project called Wikipedia. (Shirky 2008: 116)

We can still see this today on the 'Talk' pages; when one editor wants to delete something, for instance the latest update on the career of a pop star, they justify their action by saying that the offending text isn't the sort of thing one would see in an encyclopaedia. More subtly, the apparently stance-less style, the format of named topic followed by definition and then smaller sections, the attempt at universal coverage, the references, all draw on a history going back to the French encyclopaedists of the eighteenth century and to the *Encyclopedia Britannica*, even if they don't have Denis Diderot doing the writing. The project took off, with thousands of articles added every month, and hundreds of thousands of 'editors' getting involved. It also became the subject of repeated attacks in the media, more significantly, repeated attacks by vandals. It has since developed an elaborate administration system (also staffed by volunteers), but it is still possible for anyone to log on and edit almost any article.

Genres rise (usually not this fast), and they also fall as people no longer need them. Blogs are repeatedly declared to be over: 'Beyond Blogs' (*Business Week*), 'Twitter, Flickr, Facebook Make Blogs Look So 2004' (*Wired*), 'Is Blogging Dead?' (BBC). There are good points about changes in all these obituary blogs and articles, but they tend to focus on one kind of blog (diaries or political blogs), not on the larger change in reading and writing that goes with them. According to these articles, blogs are being replaced by MySpace, Facebook, Twitter, Flickr and whatever other new social networking sites have emerged in the time it took me to type these words, get them printed, and then get them in book form to you.

The always-threatened demise of *Wikipedia* is a more complex issue, since it isn't being replaced by something newer that does the same thing (rivals such as *Citizendium*, which uses expert contributors, and *Conservapedia*, which takes an acknowledged political position, can never match it for size or users, or, I think, quality). The commentators who declare 'The Death of *Wikipedia*' (in a title from Nicholas Carr's blog), and more seriously, the many devoted Wikipedians who drop out, are disillusioned with its failure to live up to the ideals they had for it. Externally, it has controversies in mainstream media about errors (see the readings in Chapter 9), and internally, it gets caught up in endless bureaucratic battles over edit wars, copyright images and administrator selection, with accusations and counter-accusations. But there is another threat: the smothering of good articles under waves of vandalism, trolling and flaming. To understand why this hasn't happened yet, we need to look at the community around *Wikipedia*, as I will do in the last section of this chapter. But first I will look at the more obvious aspects of texts in a genre: what they look like and how they are used.

2.2 What does a text in this genre look like and what does it say?

Let's start with the obvious: both pages that I have used as examples are in three columns, the middle one wider than the two on the sides, a logo at top left, some navigation devices in a bar across the top, lots of highlighted text indicating lists of links down the left side, and an image on the right. Both have long sections of written language in the middle. That is in itself surprising, because one could insert any sort of visual or aural text there, but the familiar letters and numbers that we know from the keyboard still do most of the heavy lifting.

Some genres have clear stylistic markers, such as the long noun phrases of scientific articles or the shortenings and letter/number homophones (gr8) said to be frequent in text messages. What can we find here? In the part of the blog imitating a letter, there are some traces of the sort of interactive language often found in computer-mediated texts: it starts with a question, ('You know how you used to have something going on in the kitchen . . .?') and ends with 'xo' (hugs and kisses, I'm told). Further down, in the comments, we have conversational particles ('Oh my'), typographical imitation of paralinguistic features ('I'm sooo making this'), the ubiquitous exclamation marks ('Looks delicious!!'), and non-standard use of lower case ('this is sweet!'). But that does not give us enough to define a style for blogs. Nor does the list of quantities and ingredients, followed by a set of directives, define the genre of blogs; that is, of course, a recipe.

The *Fun Home* text starts with the topic as the first words, and a definition, then a series of statements of facts, not necessarily connected to each other, with names and dates, and no direct expressions of stance (see Chapter 7). This is like an encyclopaedia article, and one would expect a different style in a wiki that followed some other genre, for instance giving travel information. Both new media carry content that could have been in earlier media, in the styles of those older media. Neither medium is defined by a particularly linguistic register, though some styles come to be favoured for some uses of a blog or wiki. If we want to find what is specific to these genres, we are going to have to look not only at the style but also at the technology and what people do with it.

2.3 How (and where and when and why) do people use this genre?

Genres aren't just texts, they include and shape practices, ways of doing things. To understand these practices, we can start with the code that makes both genres work. Blogs, like all texts on the web, are based on **HTML** (HyperText Mark-up Language). This puts in characters that enable users to write texts that can be read of any browser, on any machine, with the same sort of format (the marking-up part of the name); it doesn't require you to have some special software on your computer, as you must have for word processing in Microsoft Word, for instance. It also enables the links to other texts that we saw in the previous paragraph (that's the Hypertext part of the name). Blogs and wikis were invented by people who knew very well how to write HTML code themselves.

But they made it so that users didn't have to know how to do this; users just type, and click on a button when they want to insert a link, or make the text bold, or start a list, or put in a picture. When Heidi Swanson of *101 Cookbooks* created this text, she just opened a box in her blogging software, and typed a page that looked like what she wanted. She could go into another page that showed all the HTML codes, but she would presumably only do this only if she was having problems getting it to look like what she wanted, for instance an unwanted extra space, or italics that look funny. I don't know about Ms Swanson (she has a techie background according to her 'About' page), but most bloggers probably just type in a box, put in the links they want, and hit 'Publish'. That is why there are millions of bloggers, not dozens.

As I noted in Chapter 1, a defining feature of blogs is that these entries come in reverse chronological order; that implies readers are generally interested in the most recent entry first. But they may be interested in some earlier entry, as when I sent you to read a page posted long before you read it. That link at the bottom of the short *101 Cookbooks* text on the main page leads to a permanent page, so we always have a URL (like the one I gave you at the beginning of the chapter) that leads to that specific post, without scrolling down through everything the blogger has posted since. Another aspect of the text in use is the list of comments (52 at the moment) giving variations on the recipe and asking questions. This particular blog also has links out from the text, so you can find out more about 'Wholesome Sweeteners' Organic Molasses', and also links in to the text (which some blogs but not this one show). As we will see in Chapter 3, the use of links as part of the linking text is another characteristic of blogs, and this link text using the brand name of a product is characteristic of this author. Another neat technology in the blog is the RSS ('Really Simple Syndication') feed that will download new entries to your computer as soon as they are published.

HTML is also the basis of *Wikipedia*, as it is of every other page on the web (though wikis present users with a simplified annotation system that is not nearly so formidable looking). Most users just see the *Wikipedia* article as a formatted page, maybe something they can use to cut and paste for their homework. To see how it functions, one needs to look at the four tabs across the top of the article, below the *Wikipedia* banner. One is the page you look at first, the article. 'Edit this page' leads to a page where you can edit the source code of the article yourself, just as a blogger could edit the blog, only this page is open to anyone who is reading it, not just to the blogger(s) who have access rights. The 'History' tab lists all previous versions of the article, so even if someone has edited it since I wrote about it, you can still find exactly the version I used (14 October 2008, last edited by Jonathan Rowe of

Cheshire, Connecticut). That is also a crucial aspect of wikis, allowing a user to revert to an earlier version if they don't like the most recent changes. Finally there is the 'Discussion' tab, which leads to the 'Talk' pages, where editors can discuss (ideally in rational, collaborative ways) the changes they have made or propose to make (As we will see in Chapter 10, the discussions do not always live up to this ideal). *Wikipedia* also has all sorts of other software that make it run more smoothly, formatting tools that make it easy to insert the required references, 'bots' that check links, revert vandalism, and even create articles, 'watch lists' that tell you when someone has changed the page you have edited. But the central innovation that makes it a wiki is the user-editable web page.

One way to look at these technologies is as providing ***affordances***, aspects of the environment that we see in terms of their use (see 'What I read'). Think of coming to a door you want to go through: if there is a D-shaped curve of metal coming out from it, you pull, and if there is a metal plate, you push, even if you don't see the words *Pull* or *Push*. If there is neither, you look around, and if there is a button, you push it. On some trains in the UK, there is a button near the door, and the guards have to keep announcing on the loudspeakers that this button is an alarm. People keep pushing the button, not because they are stupid, or can't read 'A-L-A-R-M', but because they expect their environment to make sense in terms of the ways they want to use it. Someone coming to a web page expects it to be organized in a certain way, and to do certain things; we look at it as meant for use. We look around for navigation buttons, we click on highlighted texts, we roll the cursor over a picture to see if it is a link. The tabs in Wikipedia conform to our use of other interfaces, so many users will already think of them as leading to other pages 'behind' this one, like folders in a file drawer. That doesn't mean that the technology makes us act in a certain way. You can see a D-shaped piece of metal as a door handle, or you can hang a coathanger or a sign on it. The comments in blogs can be used for spam, and the editing function of *Wikipedia* can enable a vandal to have a few seconds fun with an obscene insult to a classmate. So instead of looking for technology determining uses, or people determining the technology, it is better to look for an interaction of the user, sitting at his or her computer, and a complex technology that makes some things easy and some things hard to do.

2.4 What sort of society does the genre create?

Users of these texts don't just create a genre, they create a social world. So far I have been talking about individual writers and readers, Heidi

Swanson creating *101 Cookbooks*, many anonymous editors creating the *Fun Home* article, and you the reader looking at both pages. But there are clearly lots of other people involved. In the blog, there are the 52 people who commented on the bean recipe, those who clicked on an Amazon link and made Ms Swanson some money, the people linking to it from other recipe sites – and of course the people who cooked and ate the beans, all over the world. In the *Wikipedia* article, there are the people who wrote text, corrected punctuation, found references, tried to get it all deleted, kept it from being deleted and vandalized it – and those who printed it out and took it to their book groups when they were talking about Alison Bechdel. They see themselves as doing a little bit on a specific text, but in doing so they are also reproducing a genre and shaping it. They draw on certain expectations, but they also reinforce those expectations, so, for instance, the next time you come to a recipe site you look for the comments, or the next time you come to a *Wikipedia* page about a book, you look for the template with the publishing details.

There have been many studies of the social worlds constructed on the web (see 'What I read'). On the one had, social life on the web seems pretty much like social life on my street or in my department: people gossip, buy things, build up reputations, exchange recipes, read books together, and very occasionally attack each other (verbally). On the other hand, social life on the web often removes indications of the actors' names, status and places, so we realize how much we usually rely on those indications. Usually a cookbook writer might begin with a famous restaurant or a degree in food science, something to give them status. Heidi Swanson began, by her own account, with a shelf of mostly unused cookbooks, and the commitment to cook a different recipe every day, and tell people how it turned out. She gained a huge following through readers who passed on her recipes and a link to her blog, and through broadcast and press stories telling about her project, so she was showered with requests to endorse a book, implement, shop or an ingredient. There is a lot of mockery of foodies, but this explosion of interest reminds us that a recipe was always a social genre; we didn't just want to know the ingredients and methods, we wanted to know who cooks it, who eats it – and how it turns out. The internet breaks down the boundary between the experts and the novices, so anyone can contribute. And then it draws that boundary again, so that *101 Cookbooks* and some other blogs emerge at the top of the heap. Technorati, the search engine for blog tags, uses the term 'authority' for its measure of how much a blog is linked to by others (see Chapter 8).

When Jimmy Wales and Larry Sanger went from hiring experts for their *Nupedia* project to letting in the world at large for *Wikipedia*, they inaugurated a similar shake-up in networks and status. Expertise has traditionally been centralized, in universities and professions, exams and degrees, positions and awards. And knowledge production has a centre, in research council grants, labs and journals, all based in a few places around the world. Then there is a periphery of people who want to get this knowledge, through newspapers, popular books or museums. *Wikipedia* proposes that the project of collecting this knowledge for everyday use should be put in the hands of the scattered users, not the centralized experts. So it flattens out the hierarchies; anyone can contribute, if they can keep their contributions from being immediately reverted by other editors. But *Wikipedia* is like the blogosphere in that, having flattened out the social world, it soon built up its own kinds of authority. The most obvious authority is that of 'Administrators', a few thousand experienced editors (from the millions of people who edit and billions who use *Wikipedia*) who can use special tools to resolve disputes. But to be considered as an administrator, you already have to have a less official kind of status in the world of Wikipedians, as someone who edits a lot, over a long period, usually specializing in certain kinds of edits, someone already respected by other editors. As a page in *Wikipedia* reminds us, *Wikipedia* is not a social networking site; it is not *MySpace* or *Facebook*. But each successful article develops its own community of people who recognize each other's work (though they may disagree), share some basic norms, and joke about personal skills, tics and hobby-horses.

I have said that blogs and wikis are different in their styles. They are also different in the kinds of social networks they produce. Blogs develop the personal, even then there are a number of authors sharing a site; *101 Cookbooks*, like all the best blogs, gives a strong sense of a personal voice, so even when Heidi Swanson gives a recipe from another book, it comes across with views and experience. Other blogs are similarly personal in style, even when they are discussing something usually thought of as not a personal matter, such as cosmological theories or English modal verbs (I return to this sense of personal stance in Chapter 7). We could think of each blog as one point, with a number of arrows going out to other blogs and to the various readers who comment back. Wikis like *Wikipedia*, in contrast, strive for the impersonal, everyone collaborating to produce a common product that has none of their names on it. We could think of the *Fun Home* article as a point with all the arrows going to it. Of course this impersonal front page is the result of intensely personal disputes on the 'Talk' pages; I return to those in Chapter 10.

2.5 Who owns this genre?

A successful genre – the shipping report giving the weather at sea, a scientific article reporting an experiment, a bird book identifying a coal tit – has a community that owns it. Bloggers saw right away that blogs develop their own communities. *Wikipedia* tells me that Brad L. Graham invented the term *blogosphere* in 1999; here's the original context:

> Goodbye, cyberspace! Hello, blogiverse! Blogosphere? Blogmos?
> http://www.bradlands.com/weblog/comments/september_10_1999/

As you can see, *blogosphere* was a joke (like *blog* itself), but it was picked up by serious publications, so we now have Technorati's annual 'State of the Blogosphere', which is not a joke (though there is presumably a joke in the mock-ponderous title, with its allusion to the US President's 'State of the Union Address'). The term was picked up, like *cyberspace* (coined by William Gibson in his 1984 novel *Neuromancer*), because it was a speculative concept ready to happen for real. Bloggers read each other, linked to each other, developed blogrolls (the lists of other favourite blogs along the side column). Initially, most bloggers shared a technical background (they were mostly web designers) and a North American location; now they are from all sorts of different jobs, languages and places. But there is still some sense of identifying with a movement and a mission, for instance, when one blogger defends others against criticisms from the mainstream media, or worse, the violence of oppressive states. The blogosphere can mobilize to bring down a politician, hold a corporation to account, popularize a book, spread a video – or repeat endlessly a vicious lie about a candidate, long after it has been debunked in the press.

Perhaps the community of bloggers is not so much a public sphere as a set of little *sphericules* (a term I get from Todd Gitlin (1998), multiple publics that pursue their own discussions without reference to a single unified national or global 'public' (see also Warner 2002). This idea, which is counterintuitive to people who study mass media, makes perfect sense for those who study internet communities. There is a Farsi blogosphere in Iran and beyond, a conservative blogosphere in the US, a scientific blogosphere, a Christian blogosphere. And new types of blogs have proliferated to serve these emerging communities: I have seen references to warblogs (focusing on the 'War on Terror'), milblogs (those specifically by soldiers), foodblogs, mommyblogs, lawblogs and dogblogs – yes, blogs written in the names of dogs (I mis-typed *dog blog* in that last one, and Google gave me a list of *bog blogs*, concerned with documenting toilets around the world). A look back to the origins of blogs shows that the blogosphere inherently tends to break up this way; while a television news broadcast or a newspaper article seems to address anyone (even if its actual audience is fairly specifically defined), the successful blogger writes, not for the world at large, but for people just like him or her, wherever there may be. There usually turn out to be a lot of those people, however narrow the group may be, and they turn out to be linked in complex ways. As Neil Gaiman has said in an interview, 'the blogosphere is not organized, but it's really well disorganized' (Bruns and Jacobs 2006: 253).

A sense of community is absolutely essential to *Wikipedia*. A look at the 'Talk' pages shows community at work, with shared norms, even if the definition of those norms is endlessly argued over. User pages show people rewarding others with recognition (often in the form of little primary-school stars) for their skills in starting articles, adding links, clearing up punctuation, getting them made feature articles or reverting vandalism. We will see in Chapter 9 that the community around the article on a British city, *Manchester*, included not just local historians and enthusiasts, but contributions from around the world, many of them from people who haven't been to Manchester and know nothing at all about it, but who do hate to see a misspelling or a bad link. Clay Shirky makes a telling point about the strength and vulnerability of *Wikipedia* in its dependence on this community: '*Wikipedia* exists because enough people love it and, more importantly, love one another in its context' (2008: 141). The continued existence of a print encyclopaedia depends on a publisher and paid editors and contributors; if the money stopped flowing, the books would sit on library shelves slowly going out of date (as does the 1911 Eleventh edition of the *Encyclopedia Britannica*), but they would still be useful. But *Wikipedia* depends on the ability to fight off vandals and special interest groups, and that ability depends on the willingness of a community sharing its goals. 'Were that willingness to fade, the most contentious articles on *Wikipedia*, the articles on abortion and Islam and evolution, would be gone within hours, and it's unlikely the whole enterprise would survive a week' (2008: 141). This reliance on shared effort is one reason that *Wikipedia* has been so fascinating to social scientists interested in knowledge, computer scientists interested in online collaboration and economists interested in new forms of organization.

But in celebrating this community, I may be drifting into utopian optimism that doesn't have much to do with text analysis. In fact, the world of *Wikipedia*, like the blogosphere, soon breaks down into smaller communities. There are those who develop articles on graphic novels, like *Fun Home*, and those who add bits on US counties or highways, those who specialize in the late-eighteenth-century British dissenters and their intellectual world, and those who argue over conspiracy theories about the events of September 11, 2001. More fundamentally, there are differences in the interpretation of Wikipedia itself, as shown by the formation of the 'Association of Deletionist Wikipedians' (who go around nominating articles they see as trivial or unsupported for deletion), the

25

'Association of Inclusionist Wikipedians' (who try to save these articles from deletion, often by doing a great deal of work to show 'notability') and my favourite, the 'Association of Wikipedians Who Dislike Making Broad Judgements About the Worthiness of a General Category of Article, and Who Are in Favor of the Deletion of Some Particularly Bad Articles, but That Doesn't Mean They are Deletionist'. Though the last association is, presumably, a joke, there is a serious issue at stake about the point of the whole enterprise, the Deletionists wanting the make it a limited but authoritative standard like traditional print encyclopaedias, and the Inclusionists wanting it to develop a broader concept of what counts as useful knowledge.

I started this chapter by asking you to put two texts in categories. Communities have names for the genres they use, and having such names may be part of what makes them a community. That's why the people who used weblogs seized on *blog, blogger, blogosphere, warblog* and all the variants; recognizing these classifications was part of being in the community. Other useful distinctions, like the one made by Rebecca Blood (2002c) between filter blogs and diary blogs, never got codified in names. For most people, *wiki* never became a genre name; *Wikipedia*, by far the best known application of wiki software, is what they know. Anyone who sees the *Fun Home* article calls it *Wikipedia*, not 'a wiki', just as one says one has a dog at home, or even a Staffordshire terrier, not a mammal. Whether one names genres at a more general level (*blog, wiki*) or more specific (*warblog, Wikipedia*), or still more specific (*milblog, User Page*) is a matter of what one does with them, not some general rule for naming.

2.6 Analysing emerging genres

By the time you read this, blogs may be over, replaced by various subgenres and other ways of networking. And *Wikipedia* may be going downhill (though people have been saying it was going downhill since the very beginning, and it shows no signs of going away). We will still need to analyse whatever genres emerge, using some concepts linking the forms and the uses to which they are put. To start with, we will need to look at the ways they emerge and change – processes that in computer-mediated communication may happen in phases lasting months rather than decades (for instance, the rapid development of ways of working together on *Wikipedia*). We will need to look at the forms of the text themselves, and try to relate them to their content (for instance, the careful informality in the style of most blogs). We will need to look at how people use these texts, and how these uses shape and are shaped by technology (for instance, the proliferation of links in blogs). We need to look at the kinds of social worlds created, what kinds of hierarchies (or lack of hierarchy), what kinds of distances and localities are created, what identities are available. And finally, we need to consider how they are taken up by communities, and make these communities, because that is how a genre survives, as it is reproduced by each new wave of users. In the next chapter, I will consider what I have taken as one defining feature of blogs as a genre, the use of links.

2.7 What I read

There have been many academic studies of genre, in film, literarature and linguistics. Here I have followed studies that were mainly interested in academic genres, such as scientific research articles (Bazerman 1988; Swales 1990; Paltridge 1997; Bhatia 2004). In particular, I have followed the headings of the first chapter of Berkenkotter and Huckin (1995), which are (following my order, not theirs) Dynamism, Form and Content, Situatedness, Duality of Structure and Community Ownership. Carolyn Miller, one of the key researchers in establishing this tradition, co-wrote an early online article about blogs as a genre (Miller and Shepherd 2004).

There is also a large literature on online social life. I have found the anthropologists Miller and Slater (Miller and Slater 2000) particularly interesting, and also studies of blogs (Marlow 2004; Keren 2006). I find Clay Shirky's the most useful of the many popular books in this area (Shirky 2008). Magazine surveys include Kluth (2006) in *The Economist* and Baker and Green (2008) in *Business Week*.

The term *affordances* is from the psychologist James Gibson (1977); Hutchby (2001) is a good introduction to how the term is applied in technology studies.

3 This text and other texts: Creative linking

The chapter in a sentence: Blogs are defined by what they link to and how they link, often creating witty effects that are not possible in other media.

3.1 Texts and intertextuality

I said in Chapter 1 that academics like to work with clearly defined texts, ideally with a title on top and some blank spaces at the end. All computer-mediated texts, including web pages and chat, challenge this sense of the boundedness of texts, and blogs do most of all. A blog is hard to pin down because it is typically full of links to other texts. Sometimes the text doesn't make sense unless one clicks on these links – so does that mean the linked texts (and the texts that they link to) are also part of this text? This is a practical problem for analysts of blogs; it is hard to know just what to include, and it is clearly wrong to include just the posts, as if they were collected in a bound paper volume. This chapter provides a basis for analysing those links.

Of course lots of texts refer to other texts; ***intertextuality*** is an essential aspect of all academic articles and books. For instance, in a book that happens to be on my desk as I write this (Carter 2004: p. 91), I come across the following sentence:

> As Cook (2000: 81) has commented, 'all puns, even good puns, are bad puns'.

Ron Carter has quoted what we need from Guy Cook to make his point, and we may not get out Cook's book; what we need for now is entirely incorporated within Carter's text (But it's a good book – go ahead and look it up). Compare that quotation to the references in the 'What I read' section at the end of this chapter, or any academic footnote; there the citing text may just give you a brief evaluation or hint of the relevance of this text, and you need to follow it up if we are to get the benefit. But it can be rather hard to follow up an academic reference. As it happens,

I have Cook's book directly behind my desk – a thin book with a dark green spine in the middle of the second shelf from the bottom. But almost any academic text cites works that would require some effort, going to the library, checking online journals, or maybe buying it from Amazon (or AbeBooks.com, which I recommend). This effort is one reason that academic discourse has developed elaborate forms for citation, forms that have to be taught to students, forms that give us the information we need to track down the text, and also some cues to help us evaluate whether we really need to track it down.

Academic texts were designed for libraries (even if we can now find many of them online). It is hard to do a citation that is witty in itself, if it depends on your looking up the cited work to get the joke. Blogs, on the other hand, are designed for the internet, where the reader has instant access to the cited text. That access makes all the difference in how we read them. As the verb 'surf' suggests, we don't usually immerse ourselves in a discrete text of a blog, but are carried lightly and rapidly across what we think of as an endless sea of hypertexts. This chapter is about how one blog links to another, what they link to, what they link with, and what they do with these links. Links may seem to be rather limited bits of text – usually a word or a phrase that, when clicked, sends to reader to the page indicated by the URL given with that link. But they are part of the fun or work of reading most blogs, and they can be dogged, confusing, or witty.

3.2 Who links?

The first and most obvious finding when I looked at 11 blogs (see 'What I did') is that they varied widely in how many links they used. And this variation makes a difference; a blog that has lots of links per 1,000 words, like *Instapundit*, looks like a list, while one that has very few links, such as *Raising Yousuf*, looks like a series of long entries followed by comments. As Rebecca Blood (2002c) noted, blogs split early on between those that sorted out weblinks for you with a few personal comments and those that were essentially online diaries with a few links to support them. A comparison of links per 1,000 words (Table 3.1) shows clear differences between these two categories.

This is a small sample, but there seem to be three possible clusters: blogs that use links for incidental support (less than 6 links per 1,000 words), Blogs that use multiple links as an essential part of each entry (over 10 links per 1,000 words) and blogs that are built entirely around links (the one example here with 26.5 links). We will see that these types use different kinds of linking.

Table 3.1 *Comparison of blogs with fewer links and more links*

Blogs and URLs	Links per 1,000 words
101 Cookbooks http://www.101cookbooks.com/	3.8
Bitch Ph.D. http://bitchphd.blogspot.com/	3.0
BlackProf http://blackprof.com/	1.7
BoingBoing http://www.boingboing.net/	5.9
Cosmic Variance http://cosmicvariance.com/	2.4
Dave's Blog http://unknowngenius.com/blog/	5.7
Going Underground's Blog http://london-underground.blogspot.com/	12.5
India Uncut – published by Amit Varma http://indiauncut.com/	15.1
Instapundit http://www.instapundit.com/	26.5
Raising Yousuf, Unplugged http://a-mother-from-gaza.blogspot.com/	0.8
West End Whingers http://westendwhingers.wordpress.com/	10.2

3.3 Linking to

The original purpose of blogs in 1999 was to log the various sites the user had found during the day. Since then though the possibilities for linking on the web have expanded, with nearly all major news sources on line, the rise of web marketing, and web 2.0 sites providing video and sound files. Some bloggers still spend their time surfing and call attention to 'cool sites', but now, they can spend their time writing about almost anything that comes to their heads, and assume there will be something on the web to link to for support or ironic juxtaposition. Table 3.2 categorises the sites to which the blogs in my sample link.

In the next sections I will discuss each of these main categories of links.

i. To blogs

Linking is the currency of the blogosphere, and nearly all bloggers link to other bloggers. There have been a number of quantitative studies of these links (see 'What I read'), showing how they tend to cluster; for instance, liberal and conservative US blogs tend to form two poles, referring to others within their point of view but seldom referring across to the other side. So most (though not all) of *Instapundit*'s links are to other conservatives, and many to his own PajamasMedia group:

> JENNIFER RUBIN: 'A tip for presidential hopefuls: if you want your husband or wife exempt from scrutiny, sending them on the campaign trail as your surrogate or making them a key advisor isn't a good idea.'

Table 3.2 *What blogs link to*

Linking to	Number of links
Blog	**452**
including references to own blog	123
Web pages (not blogs or media)	**391**
including	
Wikipedia	67
web marketing sites	47
organization site	29
YouTube	25
Flickr and other photo sites	21
other image or sound files	7
Google	5
Facebook	3
Twitter	2
Mainstream media sites	**230**

In the same way, *Bitch PhD* links to other feminists, and *India Uncut* links to bloggers who share Amit Varma's generally secular, free-market view of Indian politics, his intense interest in cricket, and his sense of humour. Later we will see that many of his links to friends are in the form of thanks for a tip-off about something interesting on the web.

More than a quarter of these links to blogs are to the blogger's own blog. Usually these help the reader catch up on previous comments, or on one of the blogger's hobby-horses. Here's an example of *Dr Dave* carrying on a theme:

> Further reason why reading up reference material for your own neuroscience paper is a total bummer. (*Dr Dave*)

Amit Varma has an acknowledged obsession with news stories about what he considers the absurdity of Indians' reverence for cows (though it may be odd to call that obsession a hobby-horse). Each new post on cows carries a link to the whole list of previous posts.

ii. To websites (other than blogs)

The links in this category show how far the web has evolved from being a free standing collection of pages. Here is a fairly straightforward example of a website.

> This apart, the Whingers *loved* the set. (Miriam Buether) (*West End Whingers*)

As they give credit to the designer, Miriam Buether, they link to her own website. Now compare these more complex examples:

> Pinkberry Frozen Yogurt has nothing on the frozen yogurt recipe I just tried from David Lebovitz's new cookbook – The Perfect Scoop. (*101 Cookbooks*)

The first link is to an article in the Los Angeles *Times* (I'll deal with that in the next category). The second is to David Leibovitz's web page, so it could provide information about him, his business and his books. The third link is to Amazon.

Most of the links I have categorized as 'web marketing sites' are to Amazon. Of course the links enable the reader to buy the book or CD or whatever. Bloggers may use these links as part of their income, because Amazon can pay them for people who come to it through them. But these links also seem to be the standard way to provide further information about a book, such as the date, cost, other books by the author and reviews.

I am particularly interested in these links to sites of user-contributed content (the blurring of production and usage that Axel Bruns calls 'produsage' and others call **'Web 2.0'**), because they show how blogs integrate with other, newer forms of publication on the web. Lots of blogs embed YouTube links; that is one of the ways an apparently obscure video clip (for example, buffalos and lions fighting, or a candidate making a gaffe in a small meeting) can become a global cult with millions of views. Lots of blogs incorporate photos, and some are almost all photos, using the blogs on software. A Flickr link is something rather different; it says the source of the photo is elsewhere, and the link can give credit to the photographer (as required by creative commons) for an image, or it can link the reader to one's own Flickr page, and one's other photos. There are also lots of links to *Wikipedia*, for instance to explain terms the readers might not know:

> Yet, feeling guilty about leaving my books for a minute, I compromised by ~~downloading~~ renting that <u>award-winning movie</u> about <u>John Nash</u>. (*Dr Dave*)

He doesn't tell you that the movie is *A Beautiful Mind*, but refers to it in the vague way people do in conversation ('that movie'), as if relying on shared knowledge; you have to go to the *IMDB* (Internet Movie DataBase) to get the title (and lots more). You may not have heard of the mathematician John Nash, so he gives you a link to a *Wikipedia* article. But of course both *IMDB* and *Wikipedia* are collaborative productions that rely entirely on the information and opinions of millions of contributors, with their own kinds of collaboration (as we will see in Chapter 10). So one kind of computer-mediated social network leads to another.

Just recently I have begun to see links to Twitter and Facebook. As mentioned in the previous chapter, Twitter is a kind of microblog that allows short status messages about what one is doing ('*Greg is* getting on his bike to go to work in the rain'). They can be posted easily from, for instance, mobile phones or instant messenger, so they are very easily updated. A typical use in a blog assumes readers might also be reading the blogger's Twitter:

> To anyone who follows my twitter feed you might have noticed that on Saturday I headed off to Ladyfest London where I'd been invited to give a talk and chair a discussion workshop on blogging. (*Going Underground*)

The first link just lets you know that Annie Mole has a Twitter page; the second takes you to the specific entry for that day. A link on *BoingBoing* reminds us that the Mars Phoenix spaceship has its own Twitter site, for those who want to follow its progress in real time. The blog is not a commentary on various websites, but a mediator between various other forms of constantly revised information produced by the blogger and other people, often in collaboration.

iii. To mainstream media

Many claims have been made for the radical potential of the blogosphere (and other computer-mediated communication) to undermine traditional structures of information. But my count of links confirms one of the findings of much bigger surveys (see 'What I read') – that the main source for news on blogs is still the mainstream media, or MSM, the older broadcast and print media in their online forms.

> CHINESE PARENTS ARE ANGRY, as the earthquake reveals substandard construction in the schools. (*Instapundit*)

Though Glenn Reynolds and other conservative bloggers are scathing about the bias of the *New York Times*, he links to it here, and elsewhere he and other bloggers link to the BBC, MS-NBC and the *Guardian*. And they have to; however many bloggers there might be in China, or Iraq, or on Wall Street, the blogosphere needs journalists to sort out what is news. Blogs do not replace reporters; if anything, they compete only with the commentaries on the traditional news outlets. And I have undercounted the links to MSM, since I have counted only the first link, from one blog to another for instance, and not the link from that blog that may lead to an original story on the Washington *Post* or CNN site.

The blogosphere is still firmly tied to the very 'Mainstream Media' that many bloggers mock.

3.4 Linking with

There have been many studies of what bloggers link *to*, but rather few of what they link *with*, the information contained in the text about the link. When one adds a link in blogging software, one is given a choice of what text is shown, highlighted, as the link, whether a URL, a word, a phrase or even a picture. Each blog takes its character in part from the way it links, because there is the suggestion that that tiny highlighted bit corresponds in some way to something on the site to which it leads. In my sample in Table 3.3 I find the following kinds of links, in order of frequency:

Table 3.3 Kinds of linking text

Linking text	Frequency
phrase	339
name	290
title	169
word or number	92
deictic expression	69
sentence	39
URL	34
brand name	18
image	15
quotation	6

I will discuss all these categories, but in a different order, from having the linked text less or more incorporated in the linking text. As we will see in the next section, indirectness in the link text can be used for witty effect.

i. Keeping the linked text separate: URLs, titles and names

The most obvious way to refer to a web page would seem to be to put its URL. But this is seldom used in posts by experienced bloggers, because the expectation is that the reader will get to the page by clicking the link, not by typing the address into his or her browser. Inexperienced bloggers may give the whole address because that is what they would do in other media, for instance in a handout or a printed article, as a kind of academic citation:

> According to National Public Radio (<http://www.npr.org/templates/story/story.php?storyId=4561618&sc=emaf>), African Americans recruits to the Army are down 41% since 2000. (*BlackProf*)

In some examples, the URL is also the name of the site:

> There's going to be a mass attempt at this on Friday 18th May, as advertised on www.tubechallenge.com <http://www.tubechallenge.com>, and all readers of this blog are invited to come and join in. (*Going Underground*)

Usually Annie Mole would give another text for the link and the URL would be invisible to readers; here she probably gives the URL to let readers know that there is a site of this name.

If we pursue the analogy to a print citation, giving a name or a title are the next most explicit ways of indicating a link. It's logical enough that if one clicks on a title, one gets the website or full text:

> It's interesting that the Evening Standard report talks about the advice Boris was given in his first week of tenure: 'mayor of New York Michael Bloomberg also warned Mr Johnson to get rid of any manifesto pledges immediately which looked unlikely to work.' (*Going Underground*)

> First, we have Jon Swift's (you don't read his blog? For fuck's sake, people, what's wrong with you?) delightful take on Chris Muir's Hillary-in-blackface cartoon that I've been ignoring but apparently conservative bloggers are either laughing at or wringing their hands over. Do not miss his link to the absolutely vital 'Should I Use Blackface on my Blog?' chart, which should be assigned reading for frat boys and 'I don't see color' liberals alike. (*Bitch PhD*)

In the first example, the link from *Evening Standard* leads to the specific article discussed, not the newspaper's home page. In the example from *Bitch PhD*, the name 'Jon Swift' leads to the specific post she is discussing, while the word 'blog' leads to whatever is his most recent post. Then she links with the title of a specific post; usually bloggers do this when there is something clever or mysterious about the title itself:

> CJR: Press Declares Victory, Even if Obama Won't. (*Instapundit*)
> Oh Dog, here comes another punny headline: Sari state of Ktaka polls. (*India Uncut*)

References to names can lead either to stories about someone or, more commonly, to that person's blog.

> Another friend was telling me about a class taught by Peter Reinhart where they apparently made the ultimate crackers from whole-grain flour (and various seeds, if my memory serves me correctly). (*101 Cookbooks*)

I will deal later with the most common form of these name links, for giving credit to other bloggers.

ii. Giving a sample of the linked text

The web loves **synecdoche**, the rhetorical device of referring to the part when one means the whole (as in 'hands' to mean 'workers'). A thumbnail takes you to the whole photo and set on Flickr, a still takes you to to the YouTube video. **Widgets** make it easier to embed in this way, without putting the whole text on one's own site:

> Check out this lovely animation short, <u>Kiwi</u>: [YouTube frame, not the title, is the link] (*India Uncut*)

The same can be done with a quotation. Some bloggers regularly use a block quotation that will engage readers, a 'pull quote' (Blood 2002b: 68). When the whole quotation is used as the link (not a very common way of linking), the implication is that this sample can stand for the whole text:

> BILL QUICK: '<u>Its a hell of a lot easier to quit meth than either booze or tobacco. I know. Ive done all three.</u>' (*Instapundit*)

In the example, one line leads to the whole song, in a sound file if you want to sing along:

> My kid didn't care what anyone was saying, as long as she got to sing '<u>The Sun is a mass of incandescent gas</u>'. (*CosmicVariance*)

These devices are similar to titles and names, in that they leave the other text separate, but they incorporate a bit of it into the blog text. That has a definite effect on the look of the blog, making it more like a mosaic of contributions from all over, rather than a list of citations.

iii. Incorporating the linked text

A blog is not just a list of links, like Digg or other aggregators; it usually tries to present a personal point of view. One of the central problems for bloggers is how to maintain this point of view when there are links leading away to other texts, links occurring every few hundred words (or more often). One way this is done by the blogs with the most links on my list (*Instapundit, India Uncut, West End Whingers*), is the imaginative and often witty use of linking texts that make sense in one's own text while having a more complex or different sense when one follows the link. Let's start with those examples where a whole **clause** is used as a link text:

> This is immensely cool. (*India Uncut*)

> But neither Social Security nor Medicare is a need-based or poverty program, and the vast majority of the $50 trillion long-term deficit derives from shortfalls in these programs. (*BlackProf*)

> Considering Bolli eats quite a bit of Purina wet food in the form of those little foil packs of Felix I'm sure he'd approve. (*Going Underground*)

The clause sets up some expectation of what the linked text will do, so when we turn to it, we are doing a quiz, or looking at statistics, or seeing photos of a cat eating, in terms of the blog's argument.

Phrases, not whole clauses, are by far the most common link texts. They give some indication of what will be found at the end of the link, but don't make it subordinate to the blogger's statement or question.

> Also hopefully those Laurel & Hardy style piano movers from Chiswick might be able to take some lessons too. (*GoingUnderground*)

> Indeed, I really can't think which is worse: being married to a tree, or being married into a family that believes in things like manglikness, and behaves in the manner Pande describes in her column. (*India Uncut*)

> Has *any* previous presidential candidate bothered to go talk to a Native group? (*Bitch PhD*)

My sense is that this kind of link text is more flexible, just because it doesn't set up all the expectations of linking with a sentence. In most cases, the reader doesn't have to read the linked text to make sense of what the blogger is saying. But the reader may check it out anyway, if only for what Amit Varma calls the 'WTFness' of the linked story.

A link with just a word, number or deictic expression tells the reader very little about what to expect in the linked text; the text reads entirely in the linker's voice, with a kind of annotation or addition.

> We already had a real time raffle on Sunday. (*Going Underground*)

It is perhaps not surprising that the most common word used for a link is *Link*, which serves as an empty placeholder:

> Link to NATURE page, Link to BBC Radio 4 profile of Nicholas from 2003. (*BoingBoing*)

And many of the single word links are deictic expressions such as *here* and *this* (see more on deixis in Chapter 4):

> In the meantime, if you're at your wit's end, here's a needlessly complex outline of how to make your own pet food. (*Bitch PhD*)

For more essays and Op-Eds by me, <u>click here</u>. (*India Uncut*)

FORGET THE RECESSION-TALK. WANT REALLY BAD ECONOMIC NEWS? Try <u>this report:</u> (*Instapundit*)

The use of deixis is most common in the two blogs that are closest to being lists of links, and much less common in the blogs that are read as diaries or articles in which the links are secondary. If we return to the idea of a continuum, the use of the URL to link is at one extreme (the texts separate) and the use of deixis at the other (the linked text incorporated). When we make sense of *here*, we imagine a world in which all the texts are part of this one, so the blogger can point to them from her or his vantage point. The use of deictics is one of several stylistic devices that suggests the flatness of the blogosphere, the ways different discourses, locations and kinds of authority can be brought together on the same level, in the same text, as if they were the same sort of thing.

3.5 What is the link doing?

There have been extensive studies of the context and function of citations in academic writing, and similarly, there have been attempts to classify the functions of links in blogs (see 'What I read'). Any link is classified as a practical matter by readers as they read: they decide it is either one that has to be clicked on before they read further, or it isn't. I have settled for a very simple taxonomy to start with: links

- tell us **more** of what we already know from the linking text
- provide **evidence** for a claim in the text
- give **credit**
- lead us to **action**
- solve a **puzzle** posed by the lack of information in the linking text
- tell us something **different** from the text (for instance in irony).

These last categories provide ways of being witty in blogs that aren't available in non-interactive written genres.

i. More

Functions are difficult to quantify, since the same link can have multiple functions or blur the categories, but it is clear that by far the most common function is giving more information about what is already said in the blog:

> A LOOK AT <u>Barack Obama and Supreme Court appointments</u>.
> (*Instapundit*)
> Andrew – who can sit stoney faced through anything that's sup-
> posed to be funny if he puts his mind to it – was almost on the point
> of falling off his seat at Dillie's song about <u>dogging</u>. (*West End
> Whingers*)

Instapundit's link is enough to tell us the topic of the linked text, but
we would read further if we wanted to know just what the author said
these appointments would be. The Whingers give a link to *Wikipedia*
for an instance of sexual slang, a playful move that implies the reader
may not know the term and will want to look it up.

ii. Evidence

Sometimes the information in the link is not just an addition to the
linking text, but is essential to support a statement or stance, giving
it credibility. Here is *Dr Dave* in full flow against the International
Olympic Committee:

> Forget the <u>widespread corruption, the notorious bribing</u> the less
> than inspiring list of <u>IOC members</u> (a good half of which sits atop
> one minor autocratic regime or other) etc. etc. (*Dr Dave*)

Both his links are to *Wikipedia*, which is apparently offered as a source
that will be accepted even by people who disagree with him. In the following example, Amit Varma makes a broad statement about Indian
politics, and rather than support it, gives a link to an opinion article in
the *Wall Street Journal* that presumably makes the case for him (he
wants to get on to talking about cricket):

> Just as the government <u>retains a stranglehold</u> over many areas of our
> lives, the BCCI retains its monopoly over representative cricket.
> (*India Uncut*)

Laila El-Haddad uses an Israeli newspaper, a source that will have credibility with her opponents, to support her claim of excessive violence
by Israeli forces:

> And last week, 21 more dead. Five children, a farmer, a young cam-
> eraman, <u>hit by a Flechette shells</u> . . . but who cares. (*Raising
> Yousuf*)

(The 'who cares' is of course ironic). In each of these cases, there is a
possibility of someone arguing back about a matter of fact; the link gives
an economical way of acknowledging this possibility and dealing with
it, by leaving the arguing to the linking text.

iii. Credit

Bloggers who bring together links from all over frequently credit the people who told them about the link:

> (Link via email from <u>Gaurav Sabnis</u>). (*India Uncut*)

> <u>Link</u> to NATURE page, <u>Link</u> to BBC Radio 4 profile of Nicholas from 2003 (Thanks, <u>Vann Hall</u>). (*BoingBoing*)

> <u>Flippy</u> sent me an email this morning saying, in effect, that she isn't begging for a link but since I've got a bigger readership and all y'all seem to own pets of some kind or other, I might want to post this. Since I'm too lazy to write it up myself, I suggest you click over and read what she's written anyway: you can also keep up with this pet food recall nonsense at the <u>Pet Food List</u> and the <u>AVMA's site</u>. (*Bitch PhD*)

As I mentioned earlier, these credits are among the most common reasons for linking with a name. The last example shows how they are part of the circulation of the blogosphere, with less-read bloggers giving tips to more read bloggers, and getting kin return a link that will increase the popularity of their blog. The gesture is so common that it has led to the abbreviation *h/t*.

> [h/t: <u>Too Sense: Oh, Hell No.</u>] (*Bitch PhD*)

It took me a while to figure out that this stood for 'hat tip' – a tip of the hat being a way of acknowledging someone, back in the days when men wore hats (Well, I still wear one, but I seldom tip it).

iv. Action

Sometimes the function of the link is not to get you to read a text, but to get you to do something, such as give money or buy something. For instance, in a *Bitch PhD* post on a 'Travel Justly' campaign, when you follow this link –

> You can support their campaign by reading and agreeing to a <u>pledge</u> . . .:

– you are led to a site where you promise to do such things as avoid hotels where workers are on strike, and tip the cleaners. I have mentioned that *Instapundit* makes regular plugs for Amazon; these seem to be effective:

> NOW IT'S <u>CAMPING AND HIKING GEAR</u> ON SALE: At least, it's there until I <u>point it out</u>. (*Instapundit*)

The second link leads to a recent post in which he noted that once he tipped a product, and its Amazon sales shot up, its price was doubled. The action might not be a promise or a purchase; it could just be a web search. In the following example, the blogger has been discussing a contemporary response to Andrew Marvell's poem 'To His Coy Mistress', and has noted that the contemporary poet even has a blog. He goes on to compare the two poets:

> Does Andrew Marvell have a blog? Not to my knowledge, <u>no</u>. (*Cosmic Variance*)

The linked text is just a Google search for 'Andrew Marvell' and 'blog', as if the blogger just had to check (I hope that some reader will start up a blog for Mr Marvell, who died in 1678, so while he had many genres at his disposal, he did not have internet access).

v. Puzzle

Sometimes the linking text doesn't tell us nearly enough to know what the link will do. Then we get a kind of puzzle, with a witty surprise when we click the link and fill in the missing piece of information:

> The list of the inevitable <u>grows</u>. (*India Uncut*)

But when we click the link and see a story about an Australian victory in the Cricket World Cup, the implicature is that this event is, in retrospect, so likely as hardly to need comment or description. Glenn Reynolds doesn't tell us enough to know how popcorn could be deadly, so we have to follow the link:

> I'VE ALWAYS FOUND THE SMELL OF FAKE-BUTTER POPCORN NAUSEATING, but who knew that it could also be <u>deadly</u>? (*Instapundit*)

In these examples, the difficulty of figuring out the link is part of the joke. In the following example, *Dr Dave* is plotting how to get his blog first on the list of results if one Googles 'Dave':

> Disappointingly first on that star-filled list of Daves stands, last on my way to absolute power, a highly forgettable early 90's movie, featuring its namesake US president molesting every single romantic comedy clichés in the book, living in a far, far away, fairy tale White House where, I kid you not, <u>Gandhi</u> is Vice-President (boy, did we go <u>a long way</u> since then).

The first of these links reminds us that Ben Kingsley (who also played Gandhi in the movie of that title) played the Vice-President in this movie; the second links to a satirical page on the real US Vice-President at that time, Dick Cheney. The *West End Whingers*, talking about their own influence on the theatrical world, give a predictable list with one unpredictable element:

> Their relationship with the gods of West End theatre (the critics, producers, artistic directors and more recently Natasha Tripneys Mother) has always been a bit iffy. (*West End Whingers*)

The link leads to Natasha Tripney's blog, where she says her mother's opinions are like those of the Whingers.

vi. Different

Sometimes the message in the linked text is apparently irrelevant, or is opposite in meaning to the linking text. Usually the blogger does not actually tell us this, but leaves it to us to figure out for ourselves:

> So, apparently, 'The Blogosphere is in deep mourning' and It has consequently decided to stop writing about Its cat for a day, 'in honor towards' the latest US shooting craze victims. (*Dr Dave*)

If you follow the link, you come to a blogger declaring that they will suspend their blog for the day because of the Virginia Tech shootings. As you can probably tell, Dr Dave has little respect for this action; he calculates that if we suspend blogging for every death in Darfur, we will never have to blog again. In this case, the juxtaposition of the two views (and styles) is meant to mock the linked text. The difference can also be used for self mockery. Here a blogger is discussing a topic in cosmology:

> There will be many smaller fluctuations that do just as well; the minimal one you might imagine would be a single brain-sized collection of particles that just has time to look around and go Aaaaaagggghhhhhhh before dissolving back into equilibrium. (*Cosmic Variance*)

The link is to a sketch from Monty Python on YouTube.

vii. Wit

What makes a blog link witty? Rebecca Blood talks about the 'clever link text' school (2002b: 68), and even those who don't agree with the views or interests of the bloggers I am studying would agree that most of them are cleverer than, say, me. I would say that the cleverness comes from a kind of systematic unexpectedness in any of the aspects of links that I have considered: what they link to, what they link with, or how the link functions. But to say they are unexpected requires us to have some idea of what would be expected. For that we might turn to Paul Grice's Cooperative Principle (see 'What I read' for references). Grice's approach, to which I will return in later chapters, has some complex ramifications, but the basic point is simple. It is that we can make sense of things said in conversation only if we assume that the person with whom we are talking is trying to cooperate: to tell the truth, say as much as we need to know, make it relevant to what we are talking about, and say it as clearly as possible. His point is not that people always fulfil these expectations: they lie, say too little or too much, make apparently irrelevant comments and are obscure. When the speaker/writer breaks the maxim without letting the listener/reader know, it is a ***violation***. In a lie, for instance, the speaker breaks the maxim of quality, but if it is successful the listener doesn't know. There are more interesting cases when one participant deliberately and obviously ***flouts*** the principle, the other participant might wonder why, and might draw out further, unstated propositions as intended by the speaker. Those unstated propositions (or attitudes or other information) are ***implicatures***.

If the Cooperative Principle applies to blog links, then we would assume when we see a bit of underlined and highlighted text that it will take us to the page named there, that the links and their descriptions will be in enough detail to let us know what we need to know, and no more, that the linked texts will be relevant to the linking text, and will be made as clearly and economically as possible. If all bloggers did all that, blogs would be simple lists of possible pages, without any personal intervention, rather like Digg or other aggregators of possible web pages. Much of the wit and personality of blogs comes in the flouts of the maxims of quality, quantity, relation and manner.

Quality. In the examples I have studied, blogs do not violate the maxim of quality in their links; that is, they don't lie and say that this is a link to *Wikipedia* when in fact it is a link to a different site (It is possible to lie in a hypertext link; I see that a phishing email trying to get my bank details gives a URL linking text that is apparently my bank, while the link itself, visible by rolling over it, is a different address in Poland). Blogs do sometimes flout this maxim, for instance when the link on Dick Cheney, as we saw earlier, led to a parody site about him, rather than an official information site. But no one is supposed to be deceived by this; we are supposed to draw an implicature, perhaps that *Dr Dave* thinks that the parody site is a fairly accurate portrayal of the Vice-President. The best example I have of a flout here is 'The blogosphere is in deep mourning'; the linking blogger does not believe this to be true, and expects us to see that he doesn't, and to mock the linked article for its self-importance.

Quantity. The examples in the sections 'More' and 'Puzzle' above can say too little, and the effect is witty if they say too little to understand the link text, and then the link then makes all clear (as in the links on 'inevitable' leading to the Cricket World Cup, or 'deadly' leading to an article on fake butter). It can also be witty, in a different way, to say too much. The *West End Whingers* give a link for every name and many terms in their theatre reviews, overloading us with specific information and leading to an intentionally comic effect that parallels their tendency to asides and apparently irrelevant remarks. For instance, they raise doubts about whether a British actor has taken his characterization of an American character to deep enough levels:

> Phil was unconvinced by the final beach scene in which Webb was wearing a pair of Next underpants beneath his shorts. Does Next have a presence in the US? Phil made a mental note to check but never got round to it. (*West End Whingers*)

A link to the corporate website of Next is clearly unnecessary; it shows the lengths to which Phil is imagined to go to pursue this not particularly relevant issue, once he has read the label on the actor's underwear.

Relation. The examples given earlier under 'Different' flout the maxim of relevance because the links seem, at first glance, unrelated to the point at hand. We then look for whatever shreds of a relation we can find, even if it is just the sound 'aaargh' (not the whole sketch), or the identification of Ben Kingsley (not the rest of the information about the movie).

Manner. Most of the wit of blogs is in saying things briefly but clearly. But there can also be amusement in saying things in an obscure and roundabout manner. An example of a flout of manner in linking is *Dr Dave's* account of a friend calling him in the middle of the night to get him to come over to a party where he could see the Japanese musician Ryūichi Sakamoto. Each syllable –

Sa.ka.mo.to.Ri.yū.i.chi

has a different link to a *Wikipedia* article or a YouTube video. The friend is pronouncing every syllable, as shown by the full stops (flouting the maxim of manner), to convey the implicature that Dave must have failed to understand whom he is talking about, because Dave remains in bed. Dave is linking every syllable, rather than the whole name (again flouting the maxim of manner), to convey the wide range of reasons to want to see him.

Wit: An example

Here is a whole post from *Bitch PhD* in which flouts of maxims convey a message indirectly:

(Filthy Rich) Blog Action Day

posted by BritFriend

~~I cant think of a better time to ask you to help ...~~
Actually, before I tell you about them, have a look at <u>this page</u> . . .
. . . and then guess the number that would take you below 50% . . . .
. . . and enter it . . .
. . . and keep guessing . . .
and now, I cant think of a better time to ask you to help <u>these people</u>
(who are probably in the same half as you).
Thanks.
Britfriend

We assume Britfriend wants to convey something in this post. But both
links flout the maxim of quantity, so we don't know what we will find
on 'this page' or who 'these people' are. Similarly (though it is nothing
to do with links), the blogger strikes out their first start, but leaves it in
the text, flouting the maxim of manner, and flouts the maxim again by
repeating those same words later. There is also a flout of the maxim of
quality in the title; readers are not likely to be, in their own estimation,
'filthy rich'. Then one follows the links. The first leads to a website in
which you type in your income and it tells you what percentage you are
in of the wealthiest people in the world ('filthy rich') (Hint, even a UK
university lecturer comes out well up in the top 1%). The blogger then
asks you to keep guessing at what a median income of all people would
be, presumably because you will always guess too high, and thus under-
estimate the poverty of most people in the world. Only then do they
repeat their original, struck out appeal for help, leading you to Kiva, an
organization that organizes loans to small enterprises in developing
countries. You then realize that there is a point to this indirectness; you
might not have paid any attention to Kiva if the link had just come after
a text saying it was time to give, but its relevance becomes apparent
after you have gone through the process on the first linked page. With
this indirectness, you learn something about this charitable foundation,
but you also learn something about yourself, and your own typical
response to charity appeals.

3.6 Links, affordances and innovation

There are many kinds of intertextuality in blogs: quotation of other
texts, echoing or transformation of familiar slogans and commonplaces,
picking up of new phrases or (more often) acronyms like WTF. But
I have focused in this chapter on the links because they are what make
blogs different from other genres. Links are an example of what I discussed in Chapter 2 as ***affordances***. Blogging software allows bloggers

to insert links easily, to update easily, to use all sorts of texts and images for the links, and to embed them in formatted text. In the 8 years or so since its invention, bloggers have picked up these affordances and put them to new uses, embedding videos and pictures, using all sorts of features for link text, and attaching links to almost every word or even every syllable. And the users of blogs orient to these affordances, developing a reading style that may involve moving to another text, and maybe back again, to try to figure out what the blogger is trying to say, and what stance the blogger is taking on this new text. Nothing in the hypertext link itself determines these new practices of reading and writing; they come out of millions of people seeing what they could do with these new forms. I have stressed an aspect of these practices that is often overlooked: the bloggers are playful, even on serious topics, and the readers have at least the chance of having fun.

3.7 What I did

The topic of this chapter is rather better adapted to quantitative study – counting things and comparing – than those of some of the other chapters. But it is hard work, because there are lots of links to consider in most blogs. I chose a range of blogs, some that were likely to have few links and some with lots, blogs with multiple authors and others with single authors, with comments and without. I started with a small corpus of 2,000 words for each blog, from the same period, to figure out some categories, and then added about 10,000 words from a later period of the same blogs. As the tables in the chapter show, the blogs vary enormously in the number and type of links. It's worth noting that there are very few links in comments (bloggers talk about linked texts, while commenters talk about the blog posts). So blogs that have no comments (such as *Instapundit*) will inevitably have a higher ratio of links per 1,000 words. I coded the links by what they linked to and what they linked with; the coding of functions came later, as an afterthought. I included only posts and comments; I did not include sidebars, blogrolls, navigation, or the permanent links in each post to a free-standing version of that post. Some of the automatic links on a blog, put in the sidebar by an RSS feed or advertising software, make for interesting variations on the intertextuality of a blog.

3.8 What I read

On the practical side of linking, there is brief advice in Stone (2004), and notes on the technical side in Doctorow et al. (2002); I have already quoted some of Rebecca Blood's (2002b) useful distinctions. Just as citations are one of the most widely studied aspects of academic texts, links are the most widely studied aspect of blogs. They are easy to count automatically, since every link has its own unambiguous HTML tag. Examples of studies of the complex links between blogs are those by Kumar et al. (2004), de Moor and Efimova (2004), Herring et al. (2005) and Marlowe (2006). I also found useful discussions of the kinds of links in earlier work on hypertext by Thelwall (2003) and Tosca (2000).

For introductions to Paul Grice's Co-operative Principle, see Levinson (1983: Chapter 3) and Leech (1983); Grice's original lectures are also readable (Grice 1989). On politeness, the standard reference is Brown and Levinson (1987); Watts (2003) has more recent work and Culpeper (1996) discusses impoliteness. I return to these topics when I discuss audiences in Chapter 8.

4 Place: Where is a blog?

The chapter in a sentence: Blogs usually assume a default place-lessness, but bloggers do sometimes give us an idea of the place where they are being written (for instance through pronouns or deixis) and they may do this to make contrasts, justify statements or tell stories.

4.1 Locating blogs in space and time

Where is a blog? On one level, the question is answered easily: there is a server somewhere that has this text on its hard disk, with an IP address, and cables connecting it to the internet. This conception of blog space matters sometimes – for instance when the Indian government tried to close down a few blogs after the Mumbai train bombings; since many other blogs shared the IP address of their host, the government wound up closing off almost all Indian blogs (see Chapter 8). Indian bloggers got along a few days by linking to mirror sites (servers with exactly the same information) located in Pakistan (with Indian bloggers noting the irony that they had to turn to what they see as their sometimes repressive neighbour to protect Indian freedom of speech). The physical location of the equipment also matters when a legal system tries to locate a blogger, for instance to charge them with libel or treason. But usually the IP address and physical location of the server are not at issue.

There is another kind of space, in any text, constructed by writers and imagined by readers. The linguistic cue might be as simple as saying 'Here in the UK'. In this chapter, I will look at the language choices that locate a blog in space, and give that location meaning as a place. But it turns out that there aren't many references in blogs to place, or the topic of Chapter 5, time. I don't think this is incidental; I will argue that blogs are *placeless and time-stamped*.

Blogs, set in a blogosphere of other blogs, are placeless by default; they have to do something to signal place or we don't think about it. Let's take for example five sequential posts in *Instapundit*. There are mentions of places (Vietnam, Yangtze River), but no indication of the place from which the blogger sees all this.

GETTING VIETNAM RIGHT.
> posted at 04:22 PM by Glenn Reynolds

MICHAEL VICK HAS NOTHING ON FRANK J., who's been caught running a vicious dog quiz.
> posted at 03:41 PM by Glenn Reynolds

THE YANGTZE RIVER DOLPHIN appears not to be extinct after all.
> posted at 03:35 PM by Glenn Reynolds

MORE ON THE NORMAN HSU CAMPAIGN DONATION SCANDAL, from TigerHawk: . . .
> posted at 03:16 PM by Glenn Reynolds

THE WORLD'S FASTEST barbecue pit.
But can it outrun the world's fastest port-a-potty?
> posted at 02:50 PM by Glenn Reynolds

Blogs like this don't mention where they are being written because it is unnecessary – we usually don't care where the blogger actually is right now, even if we know from the 'About' page that Glenn Reynolds works in Knoxville, Tennessee. The blogger is assumed to have an overview, able to judge the war in Vietnam, or the world's fastest barbecue pit.

This placelessness stands out because for most of our daily lives we are grounded in places, in routines of work, going out to have fun, taking care of others, going on holiday and remembering. Place in that everyday sense does occur in blogs – otherwise I would have no chapter here – and we can see it in a passage like this:

> Meanwhile, Mr. B. is off on a business trip for a week, I've agreed to take a neighbor's kids to school with PK tomorrow (must call her and find out where she lives, exactly), I've cleaned the kitchen (bonus: now I can see that the living room could use sweeping and a bit of tidying too, but FUCK THAT), and PK and I have played Battleship and spent the day in our jammes. (*Bitch PhD*)

Place here is defined by what Bitch PhD is doing – the route of the school-run, the neighbour's address, housekeeping chores in each room, the living room where one plays games, the sense of home and private space as signalled by remaining in pajamas all day. (We will return to the issue of pajamas soon.)

When I say blogs are placeless, I mean it in two senses: (1) the writing is not situated in a particular location and (2) they can be assumed to have the global vision of the blogosphere.

1. Blogs seldom name a place of writing. That's surprising because in other genres the place of origin is part of the authentication and authority of the writer and orientation of the

49

reader: think of letters, scientific articles or news reports. Joshua Meyrowitz, in his book *No Sense of Place* (1985), argues that television broke down the sense that specific behaviours, roles and rituals were specific to places. This had profound social effects, for instance when we saw rulers close up, in everyday moments, and they lost some of their distance and specialness. While television allows *consumption* anywhere (you can see the Queen in your living room), blogs and other new media allow *production* anywhere. When a television news executive described the typical blogger as 'a guy sitting in his living room in his pajamas', some right-wing US bloggers set up a site called 'Pajamas Media'. Regardless of what the bloggers on Pajamas Media actually wear to blog (I can't actually picture them in nightwear), their name claims that they can make serious public statements from what a past generation of journalists and politicians would have seen as the wrong place, not a specific newsroom in a major city but a bedroom or café or airport lounge anywhere.

2. Because of the internet, blogs see (or claim to see) everywhere at once. They are placeless in the sense of the overview discussed by the anthropologist Tim Ingold (2000), who contrasts a view of the world from within, in terms of cultural practices such as migration or farming, and a view of the world from above. The latter kind of view is visualized by the photographs taken by the Apollo 10 mission to the moon, and also by Google Earth, with its dramatic zooming back from wherever one starts, and zooming in to almost any place in the world (you will have noted, perhaps, that whole regions of the world are still rather blurry).

These two kinds of placelessness are often referred to or promised in hype about internet technologies, especially by the commercial providers of these technologies: an ad showing one can have one's office on the beach, a globe showing arrows from a computer going around the world. The default view of bloggers is like that – the whole earth (or in my sample, the whole English-speaking earth) is available at once.

The blogosphere may be imagined as separate from the geographical world, but bloggers use the language of space to construct it:

> I am immensely impressed by the quality of this discussion **over at** Marginal Revolution. (*India Uncut*)

> I'll still post **here** every now and again to refer folks to the new place. Hope to see everyone **there**! (*IsraeliMom*, on moving between one blog host and another)

In computer-generated visualizations of blog traffic (for links, see 'What I read'), the world is conceived as a vast set of points, some closer, some further, and the links between them. In this world, *Instapundit* is pretty close to *Little Green Footballs*, wherever in the world Glenn Reynolds and Charles Johnson might be, and they are both far from *Bitch PhD*, which links more to left-oriented blogs, and even further from or *101 Cookbooks* or *Cosmic Variance*, even though some of these bloggers live close enough to each other to have lunch together.

If we just took the default placelessness of blogs at face value, there would be nothing more to say in this chapter. But they do have ways of referring explicitly or implicitly to the geographical place in which they are written (such as flags, pronouns and photographs). And these indications of place do rhetorical work, such as making contrasts, justifying a statement or telling stories.

4.2 Forms: How bloggers and commenters signal place

i. Giving your home address

If one is looking for the place a blog comes from, one might start by looking at the 'About' page.

> Heidi Swanson is a San Francisco based photographer . . . (*101 Cookbooks*)

> I am a Palestinian journalist who divides her time between Gaza and the United States, where Yousuf's father, a Palestinian refugee denied his right of return to Palestine, and thus OUR right as a family to live together, resides. (*Raising Yousuf*)

> I'm a mom. I'm an Israeli. I'm other things as well, and I guess my blogging nick could have clued you in on the first two;) (*IsraeliMom*)

> My name is Heather B. Armstrong. Some of you may remember me as Heather B. Hamilton. I am married to a charming geek named Jon. We live in Salt Lake City, Utah, with our three-year-old daughter, Leta Elise, and our five-year-old dog, Chuck. (*Dooce*)

> WHO IS GLENN REYNOLDS? I'm a law professor at the University of Tennessee. (*Instapundit*)

> We work out of a top-secret bunker in North Dakota with a passel of trained monkeys. (*Sepia Mutiny*)

Places occur here as part of the name and where you're from pair that is common in conversational introductions. The place references are not always direct (Reynolds says where he works, not where he is writing now), and the author is not always there, even in place-based blogs like *India Uncut*; Amit Varma is in Mumbai, but seldom sees the need to mention it. And they may be obviously fictional, as for *Sepia Mutiny*'s North Dakota bunker, or the '*Language Log* Plaza' sometimes referred to by the linguistic bloggers. Some blogs are deliberately vague about place; *Bitch PhD* is anonymous, and though it is apparent that she lives now in California, she doesn't give this or any other identifying information.

One may not just give an address on one's 'About' page; one may do it every time one uses one's URL: for *Raising Yousuf* it is <http://a-mother-**from-gaza**.blogspot.com/>, and for someone posting a comment on *101 Cookbooks* it is <http://www.cooking**downunder**.com>. Or commenters sign themselves with a name like 'Nancy in NYC' (on *Bitch PhD*) or 'Puliogre in da USA' (on *Sepia Mutiny*). If you use a place name in the URL or signature, of course, the address identifies you even in other contexts, where place is not the issue; 'LivefromBrazil' (on *Bitch PhD*) keeps being from Brazil even when her place is not relevant to what she is saying and even when she isn't in Brazil.

ii. Naming a specific place (or not)

Apart from the URL and address, one might of course just say in the text where one is, as when Bob Chen on *Global Voices Online* says 'We live in Shenshen'. That is an exception; in my sample it seems to be assumed we know where the bloggers are, or don't care. Chen locates himself in this particular post to show that even though he lives far away from the earthquake in Chengdu, everyone in China is concerned about it.

Bloggers' posts usually invoke local place in a different way, by using place names that will only be recognized by locals, even though they may have an international readership.

> **Hammersmith** is not called Glamoursmith for nothing. (*Going Underground*)

> Even though it was a Sunday night, **Market square** was full of people hanging out. I was surprised, as I don't generally get down there on Sunday evenings. (*Instapundit*)

> My friend and I happened to be at **Mizner Park** the day that there was a design presentation at Robb & Stucky. (*Thoroughly Modern Millie*)

> In the grand tradition of <u>furthering cross-cultural enlightenment</u> that has made this blog famous in **the greater Shin-Nakano**

Sanchome area, I figured I would share some random observations about the experience. (*Dr Dave*)

You don't really need to know where these places are to get the point; the names are invoked for their associations, or even for their unfamiliarity to many readers, not for their locatability.

iii. Flying the flag

One can also state place with what is called *flagging*, using explicit or implicit invocations of nation or identity (the term is from Michael Billig (1995)). We can see explicit flagging in *Beirut Spring*, which has some version of the Lebanese flag and Cedar of Lebanon four times, and a row of faces at the top that presumably signal rather clearly his particular political allegiances within Lebanon. *Instapundit* has no flag on its masthead, but on Memorial Day Weekend, 2008, he did intersperse his links and comments with photographs showing flags in local shops, car dealers and flower planters, and even a US Mail box converted to offer a service for respectful disposal of flags that have become tattered from over-use. He doesn't wear a flag like an Old Glory lapel pin on a politician's suit (which was rather an issue at the time), but he enjoys the popular enthusiasm for the flag on a holiday. *Sepia Mutiny* has a banner rotating many different kinds of stereotypically 'Indian' images, for instance Victorian geography book images of people in exotic turbans, Bollywood stars, street vendors, gods, a hand with henna on it (try refreshing the page a few times). I think we can safely assume this is an ironic reference to the way they, as expatriate Indians or *desis*, are seen by other cultures.

iv. Deixis – being here

If I stopped here with bloggers *explicitly* naming or flagging places where they blog, I wouldn't find very much. I find more use of devices that *implicitly* suggest space. One way of doing this is the use of *deixis*, words that have a meaning only in relation to the place and time they are uttered, such as *here*, *there*, *come* and *go* (and also time expressions such as *now* and *yesterday*). Even this indirect kind of placing is unusual in the blog posts; the examples that follow are from posts in which leaving a place is the theme: in *Dooce*, because the blogger often says how she hates living in Utah, and loves visiting her old home in Los Angeles, in *Raising Yousuf*, because the topic of the blog is the extreme difficulty of crossing the border between Gaza and the rest of the world, and in *Thoroughly Modern Millie*, because she moves back from Florida to Massachusetts in the spring.

> I have been reluctant to go back because I fear that I'm going to get **there** and refuse to return to Utah. (*Dooce*)

> So much has happened since we left Gaza and in such a short period of time. If was mentally exhausting being **there**, it is even more overwhelming being away. (*Raising Yousuf*)

> Now that I've been home a few weeks I have been thinking about how different my life is '**here** and **there**.' (*Thoroughly Modern Millie*)

In these examples, they invoke *here* and *there* just because they are not posting from where they usually do.

These deictic expressions are more common in the comments, where they are used to contrast the commenter's place to that of the blogger.

> **Here** in the Uk, it is blackberry time . . . all ripening in the hedgerows and getting picked by me to be frozen, and then made into lots of crumbles and apple-blackberry pies. Yum. (comment to *Bitch PhD*)

The blogger is contrasting the blogger's Californian figs with his or her blackberries in a completely different climate zone.

> They look like the 'Potatoes O'Brien' some cafes serve **out here** in LA for Sunday brunch. (comment to *101 Cookbooks*)

The expression is rather odd, because one would not usually say 'out here' in LA in relation to the blogger, who is based in San Francisco, to the north. So maybe the commenter is placing himself or herself in relation to all the readers across the country.

> My sister **came down** to London for the weekend with my nephew last summer – they did all the touristy things: Madam Tussaud's, the London Eye, Chitty Chitty Bang Bang at the theatre and so on. (comment to *Going Underground*)

The relatives 'came down' because the blogger and implied readers of the blog are Londoners (though the actual readers, as we see, are all over the world).

> The potato based burger pattys in Indian fast food is far better, but perhaps not as healthy, as the veggie patties they sell **here** in the US of A (comment to *Sepia Mutiny*)

This example has a stress on *here* (and ironic 'US of A') because it is addressed to people from the Indian subcontinent.

We can contrast two uses of *over here* in comments to *Raising Yousuf*. The first is contrasting the places of the blogger and the commenter:

> I think some poeple **over here** (in the UK) need to see Gaza as more than just the terrible headlines; see more the people and lives behind the headlines in detail. And your blog is great at that. (comment to *Raising Yousuf*)

The second is using *here* to claim commonality with the blogger:

> what a great blog. I'm new **over here**, and I just wanted to say as a mother, and as a christian mother married to a jewish man, I love your words.. your perspective. It's very unique. I look forward to hearing more about your stories, world, and life with your darling little guy! (comment to *Raising Yousuf*)

Since I assume her *over here* is not Gaza, the expression treats Israel and Palestine as the same place, relative to wherever she was before (back there). That is certainly a possible view of the world, but it is one with which the blogger might not agree.

v. Who's we?

I had not thought, when I began coding these data, that possessives might also encode place, or rather, the first person plural possessive *our*. As with almost any use of *we*, these are vague about just how broad a group of people they are meant to include along with the writer; the *our* in the first example could be the family, or people of the Bay Area, or Californians.

> And **our** farmers markets are year round, though alas, they only go on the mornings of specific days. (*Bitch PhD*)

> How I wish the kind ladies and gents working at **our** local Barista and Cafe Coffee Day outlets would internalize this. (*India Uncut*)

> A few weeks ago, when Hillary Clinton was campaigning in Philadelphia, she began to compare herself to Rocky, **our** city's patron saint. (*BlackProf*)

> They said he was very close to a heart attack. We are so grateful for **our** wonderful public health system. (*IsraeliMom*)

> Talk about multi lingual in Switzerland, where **we have** 4 official languages and english ☺ Not to mention all the nerds (like me) talking html and php ☹ (comment to *Climb to the Stars*)

We and *our* can be inclusive or exclusive; most of these examples are exclusive, that is, they mark out a group that does not necessarily include the reader. Readers know that *Bitch PhD* is talking about her local California markets, Amit Varma is talking about outlets in Mumbai (or even one area of Mumbai), the writer in *BlackProf* speaks for

55

Philadelphians, and to non-Philadelphians, and the 'wonderful public health system' is, unfortunately for non-Israelis, only in Israel. The comment on the last example could be an exclusive or inclusive *we*; only if one reads the 'About' page, and knows the blogger who is addressed here is also Swiss, does one see it as inclusive.

vi. Two languages

It might seem odd that I left language choice to last – choice of language is often the first indication of where one is from (as people here in the UK pick out my US accent). There are large blogospheres in Spanish, Farsi, Korean and of course Chinese (which by some estimates has the world's most popular blog). But the relevant point here is that language choice does not tell *where* you are; it tells whom you want to read your text. You can blog in Farsi outside Iran or Mandarin outside China, and many people do. More interesting for our purposes are the blogs in which the languages are mixed. I marked code-switching (mixing of words or grammatical features from two or more languages) in the largely English blogs I collected. We can assume each switch occurs for a reason, and though they do not mean the blogger or commenter is in that place, they mark a kind of affiliation. So, for instance, Amit Varma, in Mumbai, drops in bits of Indian English, signalling the informality of the speech he is reporting. The Arabic greeting in *Raising Yousuf* signals a shared background as Palestinians.

> Eventually I will stumble out of the loo with only half the blood I had when I went in, reeling under an onslaught that would make Spartans proud, and some idiot friend of mine will call. '**Yaar**, don't you get bored sitting at home all day?' he or she will ask. (*India Uncut*)

> **Assalaamu 'alaikum**. 'Journalist fatigue'? I live in the West Bank, and I think that most of us are feeling this fatigue now. (comment to *Raising Yousuf*)

There is also lots of code-switching in *Sepia Mutiny*, a blog for *desis*, people who identify themselves as part of the Indian diaspora. But there is more of a risk to the switching in that blog, since India delights in many languages and it is unlikely that all desi readers will share one of them. Here a commenter who has been scolded asks for a translation, and another person who is from Anna's linguistic group obliges.

> Anna: i hope i didnt make you feel like you were being drilled and interrogated. im actually fascinated by this kind of thing, so was asking a bunch of questions. please dont take my questions as some kind of angry attack.

Kavalai padathae, kozhandai. I love that you want to know more and I didn't mean to lash out at you.

Puliogre in da USA: **Kavalai padathae, kozhandai** – translation please?

pingpong: 'Don't worry, infant!'. – Unless Anna was going for 'baby' or maybe 'babe'. (comments to *Sepia Mutiny*)

Most of the code-switching I have encountered does not tell us about the bloggers' origins, but signals he or she is comfortably cosmopolitan. *Dr Dave* (American now in Japan) responds in French to questions in French, bilingual and bi-cultural Stephanie Booth (of *Climb to the Stars*) posts sometimes in English and sometimes in French, always with a summary in the other language, and the hard-working Clotilde Dusoulier (bless her) does every post on *Chocolate & Zucchini* in both English and French (and they are followed by lots of comments in each language). She says: 'Posts for which a translation is available are indicated by a little French flag (Reminder, this is what the French flag looks like: [tricolor icon here])'.

vii. Photographs

As you can see, my textual indications of place are getting less and less direct. The last is frankly speculative. Words can come from anywhere, but photos have to have been taken somewhere, even if they only show a dog and a sofa. When bloggers regularly include their own photos, as *Dooce* for instance does (as opposed to favourites from Flickr, as used by *Thoroughly Modern Millie*), we can't help but try to place them. *Dr Dave* regularly includes 'Keitai blogs' with albums of pictures from his mobile phone, and these place him in a specific and often identifiable neighbourhood of Paris or Tokyo or wherever (as well as showing lots of pictures of his friends). The generally plain, text-based look of *Instapundit* is now and again broken up with Glenn Reynolds' photos, and on 21 May 2008, we even see him (I assume that's who it is) reflected in the glass door of 'Annie's Alterations', taking the picture. My point is that the reader doesn't need a reflection to start reconstructing the place from which the picture was taken; we do that as part of our perception of photographs.

4.3 Functions: What bloggers and posters do when they mark their place

References to the place the writer is writing have an effect: claiming an identity, making a contrast, giving a perspective on the topic, telling a story. They give both an entitlement to say things, and some constraints on what one can then say.

i. Identification – or not

Only rarely are they used the way one might expect, to claim an identity that is relevant to the topic discussed ('As an American I know . . .' or 'We Indians have seen'). Here a commenter in the US claims an identity as a South Asian, and a commenter in the prefect of Greece in which the ancient Olympia is located claims special entitlement to write about the Olympics.

> I love that story. Whenever I hear or read it, I am thrilled that **I was born a Malayalee**. (Comment to *Sepia Mutiny*)

> Angellos Makis Says: As a 'true Olympian' **born in the state of Ilias, Greece** I applaud your website. (comment to *Dr Dave*)

Such claims of identity are more common in the comments than in the blog posts. One might think the geographical identity of *IsraeliMom* is obvious enough, but she, like other bloggers, takes some pleasure in defying our expectations of the views that will go with that identity. Bob Chen eloquently states his identity as Chinese in the aftermath of the Sichuan earthquake in May 2008:

> Thrilled, panicked, confused, poor at utterance, then bursting into an emotional crack, finally into deep pathos, this mental process might have stricken a great many of the 1.3 billion Chinese in these days, regardless of the remoteness of their being from the epicenter. At this point, all Chinese are all the same. (*Global Voices Online*)

But Bob Chen does not always identify himself with China this way; his writing on *Global Voices Online* is of interest just because all Chinese are not the same, and his perspectives on the huge Chinese blogosphere tell us things we might miss. The danger for any blogger of being completely identified with a land and a people is obvious in this flaming (and misspelled) outburst in the comments against the author of *Raising Yousuf*:

> . . . **you are nothing more then** a mouthpiece for the crazy hammas loonies and idiots . . . and liveing in america yet . . .

Many of the comments on *Raising Yousuf* have nothing to do with the author or her posts, but are standard attacks on the Palestinian cause (I assume Israeli Mom deletes the worst of the comments on her blog for similar reasons). Laila El Haddad wants to present herself as a Palestinian (and also as a mother, artist, daughter, friend), but in the comments can be treated as 'just' a Palestinian. In this example, the commenter's anger is compounded by the fact that his or her target being currently in the US (to be with the father of her child), and therefore perceived as an inauthentic Palestinian and an ungrateful alien.

ii. Contrast and comparison

More commonly, the reference to the place of writing allows for a contrast with some other place. We have already seen that for commenters, the naming of a place presents the difference between this place of writing and that place of the blogger (or other commenter) as relevant in some way. When Heidi Swanson on *101 Cookbooks* has complained of the cold and fog in San Francisco, she gets the response:

> mz priss said: It was 101 degress **here in Austin, Texas** yesterday – be HAPPY to send it to y'all! (comment to *101 Cookbooks*)

The *y'all*, in a written text, is comic identification with Texas. In the following example, the writer doesn't say where he or she is from, because the name of the state is nor relevant; what *is* relevant is that it has the same law as that cited by another commenter in California.

> '. . . by California law if a tree is growing over onto public property you are legally entitled to pick that fruit. (I think.)'
> My guess is that is the law. Its the law **in my state**. Its a fair law and I would never argue the casual passerby is not completely within their rights to pluck fruit hanging in the public right-of-way. (comment to *Bitch PhD*)

In a comparison or contrast, what one has to say matters just because one is in a different place, giving one the possibility of contributing different observations, or of supporting those already made. (By the way, this last post goes on to say you really should pay the owner of the tree something for the figs.)

iii. Justification

We expect people in different places to have different ideas; that is one of the fascinations of the blogosphere. But only occasionally do people mark where they are blogging to justify or explain their stance on an issue. Here someone named Adron has joined a discussion of threatening behaviour on the tube, saying he would react forcefully, with a gun. He treats his response as characteristic of the place he is now, the US. A Londoner takes up this characterization, and uses it to reject his aggressive response.

> You guys are making me damn happy to be **in the United States**
> right now.
>
> * * *
>
> Adron – I'm also very happy you are **in the United States**, yours
> isn't an attitude I would like to see much of over here. Fimb (com-
> ments to *Going Underground*)

In these examples, place is used to explain why one holds an opinion,
but also to attack an opinion as parochial, held just by people in that
place. Place can also be used to argue that one has a special experience,
worth listening to. In the following case, the commenter says 'I live in
Arizona' as an introduction because living there is what brought the
writer in contact with what she says is the more matriarchal culture of
the Hopi.

> I live in Arizona, and I used to work with a lot of Hopi females in
> the hospitals and nursing homes where I was a nurse. (comment to
> *Bitch PhD*)

Because she knew the confidence and power of the women in this culture, she feels more qualified to comment on Hillary Clinton's campaign.

Place can also be used to account for stance in a more self-critical
way, to question the possible limitations of one's own experience, as
an explanation for differences of opinion. Here a commenter is explaining his or her suspicion of Indian Christians because of the kind of
Christianity he or she sees in the US.

> I think part of the problem might be that **those of us living in the US**
> see a very dominant/intrusive/dogmatic/fundie side of Christianity
> (especially in its reach into policy that affects all of us), so there's
> a very different attitude towards it than in India. (comment to *Sepia
> Mutiny*)

This way of putting his or her view allows the reader to believe that she
might have a different view if exposed to Indian Christians who live as
a sometimes threatened minority. Indeed *Sepia Mutiny*, written by and
for people of Indian ancestry living in the US, is especially sensitive to
the differences that place can make.

iv. Narrative

Typically a story starts with a setting, however vague ('Once upon a
time in a kingdom far far away . . .'). So mention of a place may be taken
as a signal of the beginning of a story. Here the Chicago setting suggests
that the wind described was very strong; it then leads into a series of
events and an aftermath.

60

A few days ago, a crazy windstorm/thunderstorm passed through **our Chicago neighborhood**, uprooting trees and snapping off limbs, damaging roofs, and plucking out the occasional window. I am saddened to report that our local mulberry tree was yanked from the earth by those straight-line winds. (a comment posted at *Bitch PhD*)

The comment is relevant to the main post, but in a roundabout way; the blogger had told about eating up lots of figs from the market, and this commenter was talking about picking fruit from nearby trees, so the requiem for the tree connects to the blogger's sense of the brevity of fig season. Most often, the narrative is only placed implicitly, as part of describing an action, as when Glenn Reynolds goes down to Market Square. He doesn't say 'in Knoxville', or try to characterize it as a place; even with photos, it is the background to the story of a night out with his brothers. I'll consider narratives further in the next chapter.

One of the first examples from this chapter was a snapshot from the daily life of *Bitch PhD* ('Meanwhile, Mr. B. is off on a business trip for a week'). Such stories of daily life are common in the blogs I sampled, and not just those by women. In these anecdotes, place shrinks to the space of a car or a house or a living room, but it is still present and especially meaningful. At one point in a long post about a seminar on the Naqba (the Palestinian name for the disaster that befell them in 1948), *IsraeliMom* calls a halt to the regional sweep and historical time of her discussion to get back to basics:

I think this post is getting long enough, so I'll describe the next day in another post. Time to get back to earth, clean the house, clean the kids, feed them and tuck them into bed. Back to the normal life of a mom – in the hope for normal lives for moms, dads, kids and everyone else in our region. (*IsraeliMom*)

As in this example, references to the local and the everyday can have a moral force; she is not *just* being a Mom at home, these daily activities come to stand, in this context, for the fragility of 'normal lives' in the disputed region. In my sample, the everyday trumps seminars, political speeches and news reports as the site of what is real.

v. The physical blogger

All the references to place so far are in one way or another strategic; they have a rhetorical function for the blogger or commenter. But some references arise just because the blogger, however virtual, still has a physical life. Place pins one down; one is no longer virtual and everywhere, but real, stuck in one place, and subject to all the pleasures and annoyances of being somewhere. This comes out in the example from

Amit Varma, about looking out his window. He doesn't just describe the prospect, which is consistent with the overview of the blogger; he describes the feel of the breeze, and the mosquitoes. That places him firmly in Mumbai, and those who know the city can probably place him pretty accurately on its map.

> It doesn't feel like Bombay **when I look outside my window**: there is a vast expanse of green, mangroves almost as far the horizon, and the breeze is beautiful. **Just standing by the open window** I feel tranquil-till the mosquitoes attack. (*India Uncut*)

But one doesn't have to be bitten by mosquitoes to take on a bodily existence in blogs; bloggers are always having to apologize for illness, travels, drunkenness and RSI, as keeping them from the blogging task. Here the noted linguist Barbara Partee on *Language Log* interrupts a half-serious logical analysis of the phrase 'the truth, the whole truth, and nothing but the truth', which is what one swears to tell in a US court, to note that she is about to go on holiday.

> That limits the domain of potentially relevant propositions – I'm not taking time to work this out carefully – **we're about to leave for a few days getaway** – but it narrows down the first one so that it's not about everything you say but about giving a true answer to the question. (comment to *Language Log*)

We don't need to know about her holiday, of course, any more than I need to know about the vacations of people who leave out of office replies on their email; they are reminding us of the demands and pleasures of their physical existence to explain why they are or will be away. The photos I mentioned in a previous section have the same effect, evoking even if unintentionally a specific place and time, rather than remaining in the default position of the global overview.

4.4 Place in blogs

Bloggers have the technological means to say where they are all the time, but they don't. For some of them, there is a good reason not to say: *Bitch PhD* writes anonymously, *Dr Dave* values his privacy, and both *IsraeliMom* and *Raising Yousuf* regularly comment on political issues in a situation in which there are many opinionated and dangerous potential readers. But for the most part, the bloggers in my sample don't say where they are because place is taken for granted, doesn't matter, or only confuses the issue. It is taken for granted in that regular readers of *101 Cookbooks* know that Heidi Swanson is in the San Francisco Bay area; regular readers of *Dooce* know that Heather Armstrong is in Utah; Clotilde Desouliers of *Chocolate & Zucchini* is definitely in Paris and

Amit Varma in Mumbai (or Bombay – the name is an issue). They are all tied in one way or another to a place; if they leave, they'd let us know. Place doesn't matter in such blogs as *Instapundit* or *Cosmic Variance*; they may drop a hint about a trip downtown or something, but they wouldn't want us to think that the politics of the one was just Tennessean, or the astrophysics of the other was limited to a view from Palo Alto, Pasadena, Chicago, Syracuse, Davis or Seattle (and I had to look at the 'About' page to find that information). Place confuses the issue when *The Head Heeb* wants to focus on Africa, but from New York, or *Raising Yousuf* focuses on Gaza from North Carolina, or millions of expatriate bloggers live in the blogosphere of China, Iran or India while going through their daily lives somewhere else. Mention of a place in a blog is often indirect, by use of a pronoun, a deictic expression, a word in another language, or even a photograph, rather than the name of a place. And it nearly always has a purpose, or at least an effect: comparison and contrast, justification and explanation of one's views, story-telling, or celebration of one's routine everyday world. The blogosphere may be a non-place, but it keeps getting brought down, for a moment, to one place or another.

4.5 What I did

I chose blogs for this chapter in relation to place, including six that are strongly placed (such as *India Uncut* or *Going Underground*) and six that are not (such as *Instapundit* or *Cosmic Variance*). I took 10,000 words from each. I soon found that some blogs have many more references to the place of writing than others; the cooking blogs have lots, and the politics blogs few. Posts have rather few references, and comments many more, for reasons I discuss in the analysis; that means that the blogs that don't enable comments provided much less data for this chapter. I coded them using Atlas-ti, and the categories that followed emerged gradually, as I noted them in the text.

4.6 What I read

Let's start with some provocative books on the experience of place, quite apart from blogs. One might compare the 'placelessness' that I discuss here to the 'non-places' of Marc Augé's readable book (1995) on our experience of motorways, airports and other transitional spaces. The reflection on different ways of seeing the earth, from outside and as lived experience, comes from Tim Ingold (2000). The distinction between flagging nationality and conveying it in other ways comes from Michael Billig's book *Banal Nationalism* (1995). Both Augé and

Ingold are anthropologists; Billig is a social psychologist. I found useful orientations to the study of space and place in the anthropologist Keith Basso (1996), and geographers Doreen Massey (1994) and Nigel Thrift (1997), the social psychologist John Dixon (Dixon and Durrheim 2000), and the sociologist Emanuel Schegloff (1972). There are useful ideas about place and the internet in Daniel Miller's and Don Slater's ethnographic study in Trinidad (2000). As you can guess from the dates, none of these people has anything to say about blogs.

Among linguists working on place, the most useful studies are by Ron and Suzie Wong Scollon (2003) from the perspective of semiotics and Barbara Johnstone from the perspective of sociolinguistics (1990). I have lots more references in an article on how people say where they are from in group discussions (Myers 2006).

Deixis is an important topic in the study of language; for an advanced introduction, see Levinson (1983: Chapter 2). There are interesting treatments of the strategic uses of pronouns by Mühlhäusler and Harré (1990) and John Wilson (1990).

5 Time: Now and then

The chapter in a sentence: There is more to the time of a blog than the time and date stamp; bloggers use complex references to time to give the present moment its meaning, for instance in showing the news value of the text, telling stories and projecting hypothetical futures.

Good Morning America is in my house right now standing behind me getting video footage of how badly I type. It's the standard shot of the blogger blogging, and if the producer got back to the studio in New York without this footage her boss would be all HOW WILL WE KNOW SHE IS A BLOGGER IF YOU DIDN'T FILM HER BLOG-GING? (*Dooce*)

At the bottom or top of every blog post is a date and sometimes a time, in the case of the post I have just quoted, *Thursday, 24 April 2008*. While we are often unsure about where a text was written and posted (probably Salt Lake City, Utah, here, but she doesn't say), we are never unsure about when. And we always know which post was written first in relation to another, because they are automatically arranged in reverse chronological order.

The type of precise clock time used in this blog is just one of the ways time can be indicated in blog posts; the various ways of alluding to time can give a perspective on this present moment, recall the past, maybe the immediate past, to project future events, tell stories, imagine hypothetical events, and follow the seasons and cycles of life. In this case, Heather Armstrong is blogging for the cameras, so a film crew will have a continuity shot they can use of her actually at the computer; it is a 'standard shot' of the activity of blogging in general, as if blogging were in present continuous ('I am blogging'), just now. This grounding in the present allows Armstrong to go off into other times: she imagines a future in which the film crew is in New York, and the boss there projects a still further future in which the crew imagines the response of an audience then, if the shot were (contrary to fact) not being done now. And all this time travel starts just because the camera is forcing her to focus on the present activity of typing.

5.1 Time-stamp time

Look back at the five posts from *Instapundit* at the beginning of Chapter 4. Each is followed by a date-and-time stamp, so we know the post on a political scandal comes just 6 minutes after the link to the dolphin, while Vietnam comes more than 40 minutes later, and we can follow his day more or less from getting up (early) to going to bed (late). The time-stamp gives us, not his experience of time, but a uniform and universal ticking off of clock seconds.

Bloggers can ignore this time-stamp. But they can also use it to convey the urgency and immediacy of what they are writing, as when *Cosmic Variation* has entries by all the contributors, all over the US, throughout the day that the Large Hadron Collider was turned on in Switzerland. It was a big event for them, and they wanted to convey the way they were following every minute. A Chinese blogger quoted by Bob Chen on *Global Voices Online* also uses exact times to log the activities of citizens tracking down fraudulent use of relief tents:

> 11:50 am, latest news: our first reporters have been in the community, ready to work, taking pictures of these 'bad men'. According to the clue from netizens, some one has blown the gab so that one tent has disappeared, while another remained . . . (The owner was not found). Where are they from? Bought? Embezzled? (*Global Voices Online*)

Amit Varma uses the time-stamp to construct a complex, constantly changing account of what happened in the bombing of trains in Mumbai (see Chapter 8). Since blogs are what is said at the moment, they are also constantly open to revision. The usual convention, referred to by bloggers themselves, is that one should not change what one has written once one has posted it. Instead, one might do as *Instapundit* does with new information after a story about a dubious home purchase by a California politician:

> UPDATE: An update says that Richardson denies the story. (*Instapundit*)

Glenn Reynolds of *Instapundit* uses updates a lot, and they help convey the sense that his short, pithy posts with links convey just what is happening at the moment. The strikeout font can also be used to show changes in a witty way, leaving the earlier version visible, as in this opening of an 'About' page:

> Chocolate & Zucchini is a blog written by **Clotilde Dusoulier**, a ~~24 25 26 27~~ 28-year-old Parisian woman who lives in Montmartre. (*Chocolate & Zucchini*)

The present moment, measured in clock time, and marked by the automatic time-stamp, is the default time of blogs, as placelessness is the default spatial orientation. But that doesn't mean blogs stick to the breathless flatness of the present and the regularity of clock time. There are various ways we can think of time. The time-stamp makes us think of a series of uniform divisions – days, hours, minutes, seconds – that mark off units of time in a linear fashion: It's 7:30 am. This concept of time contrasts with a relational view, in terms of the links or movements between moments: it's time to go to work. This relational sense of time is often closer to the way we feel it and live it.

5.2 Lived time and how to show it

The relational kind of time is signalled linguistically in many ways, in verb tense and aspect, in deictic expressions, in names of days or seasons, in links to events, and in adverbials that say how the time is relevant to an action. Let us return to the quotation from *Bitch PhD* at the beginning of Chapter 4:

> Meanwhile, Mr. B. is off on a business trip for a week, I've agreed to take a neighbor's kids to school with PK tomorrow (must call her and find out where she lives, exactly), I've cleaned the kitchen (bonus: now I can see that the living room could use sweeping and a bit of tidying too, but FUCK THAT), and PK and I have played Battleship and spent the day in our jammes. (*Bitch PhD*)

The post has a time-stamp, as they all do, but it also indicates time in other ways: the relational adverbials (*meanwhile, for a week*), the present perfect aspect (*have cleaned, have played*), the projection of possible future events in a deontic expression, that is, an expression of what ought to happen (*the living room could use sweeping*), and a metaphor of time as money: *spent the day*. Here time is defined as one moment before or after another, or as a duration of an activity. One event leads to another: Mr B going away leads to Dr B doing the school run; cleaning the kitchen doesn't lead to cleaning the living room.

Bloggers can also construct time by using devices that link two events. Here Annie Mole is using the present continuous, as Heather Armstrong did, but she is tying together to events, typing and rain.

> I'm typing this **as the rain is coming down with a vengeance outside** which makes the idea of a <u>Sunshine Garden</u> and <u>gardening for drought</u> seem somewhat farcial [*sic*] right now. (*Going Underground*)

Grammatically 'as the rain is coming down with a vengeance outside' is an adverbial that gives a circumstance relevant to the main clause – 'I'm typing'. It is that circumstance that makes the blogging about drought seem ironic. More flippantly, a commenter on *BoingBoing* looks back to an earlier comment and link that apparently kept him up late looking at stuff on the web, resulting in the cry of anguish that begins the comment:

> Ant @50 – Aaaarrrgggggghhhhhh!!!!
> I was going to go to bed **about 15 minutes ago**, but NOOOOO, I had to stay up a few minutes more to see what my pals at BB were up to. Never again I tell you!

As often happens in blogs, the dismay is not just reported, but enacted (*Aaaarrrgggggghhhhhh!!!!*), and the reference to his or her own activities (going to bed) is part of this enactment (I might warn you that the advice about not looking at *BoingBoing* just before bedtime is well taken). The adverbial can give the meaning to the here and now by linking it to another event:

> So much for the pictures. **In a about ten minutes from now** the sirens are going to go off marking the beginning of the Memorial Day. (*IsraeliMom*)

This conveys more of the emotional sense of waiting for the sirens than just saying, what is also true, that it is 7:50 pm on Tuesday, 6 May 2008.

The devices that indicate the writer's time are similar to those that indicate the writer's place. Time words such as *now* and *yesterday* are examples of **deixis**, just like space words such as *here* and *come*, because their meaning can be determined only when one knows the context of utterance (see Chapter 4). Time and space deixis often occur in the same sentence, as we saw in an example in the last chapter:

> It was 101 degress **here** in Austin, Texas **yesterday** – be HAPPY to send it to y'all! (*101 Cookbooks*)

One could of course say this in non-deictic ways: 'It was 101 degrees in Austin Texas on 20 May 2008'. But the deixis stresses that the writer is there, and that she experienced it, recently, and is writing now with that experience in mind.

5.3 Functions of time references

Since the moment of posting is already indicated automatically on a blog, when the blogger refers to the time of writing, he or she has a specific reason for doing so, such as stressing the importance of the present moment, telling a story, or placing events in a larger context.

i. Nowness

Some of the time references we have been considering emphasize the present moment, either because of its importance or its relevance to some assertion. *Just*, in this sense as 'at or just before the present moment', is a good example of this emphasis on the present; it adds to the news value of whatever is reported.

> I **just** got a phone call from a friend, and when she told me she was calling from Switzerland, I could feel myself starting to talk louder and louder until I was screaming, just in case she couldn't hear me *all the way over there.* (*Dooce*)

This says that the anecdote is particularly relevant because it happened very recently. A report of recent viewing and reading takes on additional significance when it is related to current events at the bloggers home in Gaza:

> I watched a little bit of 'Escape from Alcatrez' **the other day**. Funny, but it looked like paradise compared to Gaza **now**. I also **just** finished reading Ben White's 'Brief Encounters with Che Guevera', a collection of short stories, many of them about Haiti and US involvement there. Naturally, I thought of our situation. (*Raising Yousuf*)

Just, used this way, occurs far more often in the comments than in the posts:

> I **just** saw a recipe recently for polenta croutons, but I haven't tried it yet! (*101 Cookbooks*)

> I **just** discovered your website and am so excited about it! (*101 Cookbooks*)

> How serendipitous, I **just** watched something on this via the History Channel (or similar) . . . (*Sepia Mutiny*)

Someone posting a comment needs justification, and the signal *just*, indicating that it is a recent event, perhaps an apparent coincidence, serves to claim interest for what one is adding.

Other deictic time expressions are used to stress something important about the moment:

> **This morning**, I sat through the last written test of my life. (*)
> (*Dr Dave*)

The adverbial is at the beginning, what Michael Halliday calls thematic position, the 'point of departure' for the clause (Halliday 1985: 38).

I don't think it would work as well at the end of the sentence, where it would still indicate the time of the exam, but wouldn't suggest this time was the point of the announcement (The asterisk, by the way, leads to a self-deflating footnote in which he reminds himself he still has a lot of other coursework work due). Heather Armstrong tells a story about buying an expensive coffeemaker with her husband to celebrate 5 years since their wedding.

> Except, **today**, the actual day of our anniversary, that new coffee machine is sitting on the countertop in our kitchen 100 miles away, because **yesterday** we decided to drive out to my mother's cabin in the middle of the high desert. (*Dooce*)

Of course she does not need to say *today*; if she says the coffee maker *is* 100 miles away, we will know that is true at the time of writing. The *today* emphasizes the irony that they can't have the coffee from the anniversary machine on the very day of their anniversary (her family of observant Mormons doesn't drink coffee, and anyway the machine is too big to take along). The word parallels the *yesterday* that signals their change in plans.

A reference to the present moment can make one's comment more relevant; it also be used to opt out of commenting on an issue. Here Geoff Pullum is opting out of giving a full treatment of double modals (for my take on modals, see Chapter 8):

> As a member of a distinguished department of Linguistics and English Language, I might be assumed to have done some research on their origins in their emergence in the American South or their possible antecedents in the British Isles; but I have not. I am off duty **at the moment**. (*Language Log*)

Of course linguists do not go 'off duty' like police officers (least of all Professor Pullum, a prolific popular essayist). Along with the mock-pomposity of the opening, it signals a joke: even Geoff Pullum can't be an academic specialist on every linguistic topic on which he would like to blog.

ii. Narrative

Everyday stories typically start with an orientation, including place and time (see Chapter 4 and 'What I read'). They then typically go on to some Complication, and an Evaluation of the action, explicit or implied (which is why I will come back to narrative when I talk about stance in Chapter 8). This pattern is so well established that a time reference ('A long time ago . . .' or 'Last Saturday night') can seem to cue narrative, just as we saw that place references ('in a kingdom far far away') did in Chapter 4. So when *Dr Dave* says he hasn't been to the doctor much in Japan, and then says 'this morning', we know we are in for a story.

> **This morning**, though, I had to check in at my neighbourhood clinic and undergo a whole series of health exams. (*Dr Dave*)

And sure enough, he tells a humorous series of events, starting with a description of the place, complicated by the cultural differences, and ending with an ironic evaluation:

> By all means, don't miss this once-in-a-lifetime tourism opportunity next time you are in Japan.

But narratives do not need an explicit orientation in time; just a shift in tense can do it. Usually narrative uses past tense, which is why there is a time orientation at the beginning. But there is a narrative present tense that creates vividness by treating the event as if happening right now. Here is a whole post:

> **This episode features small quantities of learning**
> Leta is pushing a heavy toy down the hallway when the far side of it bumps right into Chuck's back. He's been sleeping on the floor, and although Leta keeps nudging him with the toy he won't move. She finally screams, 'CHUCK! MOVE, PLEAAAAAASE!' Isn't that considerate of her to ask so politely.
>
> Chuck thoughtfully considers her request, pulls himself off the floor and steps to the right allowing her plenty of room to pass. She sits there stunned for a second and then muses aloud, 'I <u>love</u> Chuck.'
>
> No one is more surprised than she is at this realization. (*Dooce*)

These events (unlike those in the first example in this chapter) are probably not going on before her as she types; that would usually be indicated with present continuous. It is a simple story because it has just three parts: there is an obstruction, it is removed, and the girl makes a comment on it. But it has lots of diversions along the way. We have to go back a bit in time to get the circumstances of the story ('He's been sleeping on the floor . . .'). The teller turns to us, and comments ironically on the shouting ('Isn't it considerate . . .'). As with many everyday stories, the ending comes twice. The first punchline is Leta's comment. Then we get her mother's reflection on this comment. *Dooce* does this in almost every post, and it works, I think, just because it is so economical.

Narratives can be contained in various forms of disguise. For instance, here *Dr Dave* tells an anecdote about what happened when he forgot his keys last night:

> **Life Lessons #23421, pt. 1 to 4**
> 1. If you are heading for a night out and contemplate leaving your winter coat at the office: consider double-checking said coat's

pockets for any items that you may need, further down the night. Special attention probably needs to be paid to small, flat, key-shaped items, which may turn up crucial when you finally decide to hitch a cab-ride home and find yourself very stupid, standing at your frontdoor.

You can already tell what happened. Instead of retelling these not very surprising events as a story about him, last night, he constructs them in the form of a lesson, with a generic *you* reader, generalized descriptions ('small, flat, flat key-shaped items' rather than 'my keys'), and present tense events that might potentially happen at some point. We then reconstruct the events from these lessons (This is point 1 of a 4-point list, that is itself presented as part of a much longer list of lessons he has learned). When we get to point 4, we find it is a good idea to leave a set of one's keys with a neighbor who won't mind being woken up, rather than with an ex-girlfriend – probably a useful piece of advice. He only admits explicitly that these events are what happened last night when he later addresses the helpful neighbour and promises a dinner out to compensate for her getting woken up. The success of this device depends on our being so used to such stories that we can construct them ourselves from this self-mocking, indirect form.

iii. Hypothetical and future narratives

We have seen that narratives can be constructed from the slightest hints, usually with a shift in place or time. Two or more events get put in a causal order that allows us to draw evaluative conclusions. We are so good at doing this that bloggers can offer us events in the future, hypothetical events, or even frankly implausible events and we will construct the narrative. Heather Armstrong uses hypothetical narratives particularly often, in *Dooce*, so I will take some examples from her. One reason she keeps shifting to the future is that she presents it as in part a diary about her daughter Leta, who was 3 and then 4 years old in the weeks I sampled. Once a month there is an entry addressed directly to Leta's older self.

> 15 years from now you're going to read this paragraph, here where I tell you that your favorite thing to say is DONKEY BELLIES, and whenever you say knock-knock, and I say who's there, you scream DONKEY BELLIES, and then you gasp for air as the giggles get lodged in your throat, you're going to read this and then call me and go THERE'S NOTHING FUNNY ABOUT DONKEY BELLIES. And then you're going to ask me for money. (*Dooce*)

This is a very complicated bit of projection of the present into the future. One story is about something that happens repeatedly in the present, and that is funny only because it happens repeatedly, the 4-year-old laughing at her favourite word, described down to the physical detail of Leta being overcome with her own laughter. All this is embedded in another narrative of Heather Armstrong writing this entry now ('here where I tell you . . .') and Leta reading it 15 years from now. That makes Leta 19, so it is assumed that she has moved away, so she has to phone her mother. She is given hypothetical reported speech ('THERE'S NOTHING FUNNY . . .'), which is also what we might say. Then she asks for money. Why? Because that is what generic 19-year-olds do. She has no future character except that of the typical child growing up. If this is funny, it is because the imagined future Leta rejects the fascination with the actual present Leta that is one of the reasons for the blog – she doesn't get the point, or share the implied evaluation (that this is cute behaviour).

There are many examples of such hypothetical and future narratives in *Dooce*. But they are surprisingly common in other blogs, as when a commenter imagines a future way of preparing a recipe from *101 Cookbooks*, *Bitch PhD* imagines what she would say to her child's teacher, *Going Underground* invites entries in a competition, *Dr Dave* presents starting his PhD as part of a plan for world domination, or an astrophysicist in *Cosmic Variance* imagines a cosmology in which time runs backwards. In every case, these projections of hypothetical or future events are part of an implied evaluation or description of the present.

iv. Seasons and cyclical time

A narrative about one time can also take on meaning when it is related to a cycle of recurring events, a recognition that that what happened before is happening in its regular way again (We saw that with Leta in *Dooce* telling the same knock knock joke again and again). Seasons are a key cycle binding entries into a larger narrative, for a food blogger looking for fresh peas, a retired person spending winters in Florida and summers in Massachusetts, a mother living in a desert recognizing the small change in personal routine that marks the new season, or a fan noting the opening of a new sporting season:

> **This morning**, as I dragged myself out of bed, I realized that what I need is ice coffee rather than the hot version of the beverage. That's when it dawned on me – **it's June** and **it's officially summer time!** Mornings are too warm anymore for a hot drink, so we're switching to ice coffee! (*IsraeliMom*)

> I hope it gets warmer by the time you get back. Red Sox opening day is **tomorrow** so that's a sign of Spring. (Comment to *Thoroughly Modern Millie*)

These bloggers and commenters assume that cyclical time of seasons is recognizable to all readers, even if the seasons where you live are not exactly the same as those in Israel (the heat) or Massachusetts (the baseball). Other cycles are particular to the blogger's home life, work life or health:

> **Each time** I go through a bad bout of RSI, I can be certain that my speech recognition setup breaks down. **This time**, my microphone died, and I had to buy a new headset, which seems to be working correctly, **as you can see**. (*Climb to the Stars*)

Stephanie Booth presents this event as recurring; I am told that it is indeed one of the annoying aspects of Repetitive Strain Injury (RSI) that the pain in one's arms comes and goes instead of getting progressively better. First she makes an ironic connection between two logically unrelated events: (a) the pain and (b) the failure of the speech recognition device; she needs to use her computer when this pain occurs. Then she focuses on this present occurrence, in which the narrative connection between two events is made by the modal 'had to' (again, see Chapter 7); the failure of the microphone makes it necessary and predictable that she will buy a new handset. Finally she connects this sequence to another present moment, the time in which we read the post; since we can see it on our screens now, the speech recognition system must have worked at the time she wrote the post. And, the implication is, the whole thing happens again the next time RSI strikes her. So she doesn't just convey the information that she is having this attack, and this computer problem, but she is still blogging; she also conveys the sense of 'here we go again'.

v. Historical time

The examples so far suggest that blogs construct meaningful time by linking to everyday experience, especially experiences such as growing kids, changing seasons and late nights drinking that might be shared by readers. That is what we would expect from the origins of blogs in personal diaries and lists of links. But very soon after the invention of blogs, some bloggers began to put their daily observations in a larger context of what they saw as historical events. *Instapundit* and *Little Green Footballs* started as personal observations on many topics, and only became 'warblogs' after the events of September 11, 2001 gave them what the bloggers saw as an urgent function, to comment on all sorts of political events in the light of US security issues. Similarly, *Where is Raed?*, *Baghdad Burning* and other Iraqi blogs had no choice but to make the invasion of Iraq their main (but not sole) topic. *IsraeliMom* began as a personal blog; the focus on peace in the Middle East came gradually. *Bitch PhD* is about daily events, but followed the Obama campaign; *India Uncut* contains various observations and cricket reports, but when the bombs went off in Mumbai, it became a newsblog (see Chapter 8). Perhaps the link between personal experience and wider political events is made most strongly in *Raising Yousuf*, subtitled *A Mother from Gaza*. An anonymous poster takes an explicitly historical perspective:

> I left Gaza **in late June** after spending three years there and I can't recall it as bleak as it is **today**. I've been to Gaza numerous times, but **this period of history** is very different. I just don't know how long Gaza can function. You have brother fighting brother! Never in my wildest dreams I thought this would happen. Society is being destroyed from the core and I don't know if it can ever be patched up. 1:42 PM

Comments on history in blogs tend to use this sort of exclamatory style, because bloggers are stuck inevitably in the present moment, without any real foresight or reflection. They are perhaps most effective when they focus on the ordinary. Here Bob Chen on *Global Voices Online* finds poignance in photographs of kids playing in schoolyards in Sichuan, where the 2008 earthquake destroyed so many schools.

> And the following pictures were taken **exactly one day (7 hours, actually) before** the earthquake.

They are of course not much different from pictures of any schoolyard at any break-time; the emotions are called up by our historical awareness of what happened next.

5.4 Twitter and time travel

Blogs are uniquely time-bound. Of course other genres – newspaper articles, legal documents, scientific reports – carry a date of writing, signing or publication. But blogs are automatically stamped with a date (and usually time), and arranged only in reverse chronology. Even if one wants to break out of this order, the blogging software can only give you an update or a link to what was said before. An extreme example of this time-binding is Twitter (invented by Evan Williams, who created the first widely used blogging software), where one only answers the question 'What are you doing now?' The reason blogs are not stuck in the eternal present continuous of Twitter is that bloggers can construct other times, with adverbials, time references, dates and seasons. These constructions nearly always serve a rhetorical purpose, showing how what I am saying or doing now takes on its meaning from what did happen, could happen, might happen, will happen. Time shifts can be used seriously (for instance in updating breaking news) or playfully (for instance in imagining unlikely events). Like the shifts in place, they work because we are good at telling, and listening to, stories, and we are willing to start them at the slightest hint.

5.5 What I did

I used the same passages from blogs as in Chapter 4, and coded them for different ways of presenting time. We have seen that some blogs had many more of these shifts. They were least common in blogs making general political observations (*BlackProf*) and most common, as we have seen, in blogs that use a lot of narratives (*Dooce* and *Dr Dave*). I was surprised to find that such shifts were also common in the scientific discussions of *Cosmic Variance*, where the longest entry discussed counter-intuitive cosmology in which the arrow of time can run backwards as easily as forwards.

5.6 What I read

For general theory on social science and time, see Barbara Adam (1998). On the presentation of time in discourse, see Chafe (1994), Renkema (2004: Chapter 7), and for useful observations on time adverbials, see Biber et al. (1999). There is a larger literature on everyday narratives; see for instance Polanyi (1985), Eggins and Slade (1997) and Georgakopoulou (2006; 2007). On the wider issues of how discourse is situated in historical relations, see Wodak (2001).

6 Audiences: A checklist on engaging readers

The chapter in a sentence: Bloggers use a range of devices, direct and indirect, that can make readers feel like they are being talked to, included in a group, and involved in the blog.

Blogging software means that anyone with access to the internet can post their thoughts, links and photos on a blog. But a blog does not guarantee an audience; the vast majority of bloggers get along with just a few people looking at their work, and that may suit them just fine. The handbooks on blogging suggest ways of getting more links and moving up the indexes so that people notice you. That is not what I am doing here. I am going to point out the ways that the blog texts that I studied signal engagement with their readers, from the obvious (such as using *you* a lot) to the less obvious (such as requiring readers to draw inferences that can only be made with specific shared knowledge). Some of these devices are familiar from any other genre that depends on its readers or listeners: political speeches, advertising, newspaper columns, personal letters. Other devices are developed more highly in blogs, where the writing is often highly informal and personal, but the readers can be complete strangers anywhere in the world. Bloggers create an audience-in-the-text that may not be the same as their actual audience, but which provides an impression of a friendly but sometimes mocking circle of people who share the bloggers' interests and views.

6.1 Footing: Different ways of being the audience

We should start by noting that audiences of written texts can be more complex than, say, a person at the other end of a phone, or a group of people in a theatre. A lot of linguistic analysis deals with a single speaker talking to a single hearer. But as Erving Goffman pointed out (see 'What I read'), there are several possible *footings* on each side of an actual interaction. To give a non-blog example, take, for instance, the press secretary talking at a White House press conference. In terms of *production format*, she is the **animator**, actually speaking the words. But she is speaking in the name of someone else, the US President, who is in Goffman's terms the **principal**. And while she may have chosen the words herself, they may have been chosen by others on the team, so there may be an **author** distinct from the animator. On the *participation* side, she may be directly addressing the correspondent for the *New York Times*, who had just asked a question and so would be a **ratified participant**. Other correspondents and officials in the room would be **bystanders**, not addressed but obviously there, taking notes. But the whole performance is also done for the cameras, and for us watching in the broadcast audience as **overhearers**, not addressed participants, but clearly part of the interaction.

The study of footing clearly complicates the analysis of audience in blogs. Let's take an exchange between two people on a *LiveJournal* network devoted to anorexia. One person with this condition is addressing another person with the same condition, personally, and giving advice or moral support; this other person is addressed and treated as a *ratified participant* in the interaction. But they both know there are other possible readers (*bystanders* in Goffman's terms), the registered members of this *LiveJournal* group; they have signed up giving their weight and height statistics, so let us assume that they may be strangers, but they are also self-identified anorexics. They know their words could also be read by a much wider group of people, since there is no registration needed to read the discussion; it could include parents, doctors, teenagers, journalists and many people who do not meet the weight and height criteria, all of whom are *overhearing* (metaphorically speaking) or, to use a term Goffman might have liked, *lurking*. Thus a writer might, for instance, give advice on body image meant for an Ellie, but also with the intention of projecting the right identity to the close group of regular participants in the site, and this might have, intentionally or unintentionally, a very different effect on a journalist writing a sensational piece about pro-anorexia websites. In fact, the intent to shock outsiders might be part of what keeps the inner group together. This is a particularly charged example, because the criteria for being a ratified participant are so clear. But the issue of multiple audiences (and, more subtly, multiple principal/authors/animators roles in producing the blog text) arises in many other blogs.

6.2 Address

I am using **address** here to refer to the explicit mention of the intended audience in the text. US Presidents do this when they begin a television speech with the words 'My fellow Americans'. Of course not all Americans are watching, and lots of people are watching who aren't Americans, but this beginning signals the audience for whom it is formally intended. This sort of named addressee is common in the comments on blog posts, where a commenter may need to pick out one of the dozens of people in a discussion for a response, or as in this case, to show she is responding to the original post:

> **Bitch**: I completely agree that the thought of raising a child single-handedly is far more daunting than it ought to be – especially in a nation with as much wealth as this one. (*Bitch PhD*)

'Bitch' here addresses the blogger *Bitch PhD*. This kind of direct address is rather rare in the blog posts I studied; it is used usually when the blogger wants to identify a particular subset of the audience. Here the blogger has been presenting her system for making up comical excuses for delays on the London underground:

> If you've [you're] **a driver, or train operator or customer service platform assistant or whatever** – you might be able to send me some more delay excuses, sorry perfectly rational reasons that I can drop in over time. (*Going Underground*)

Annie Mole imagines who might provide more information, and then she also enacts a bit of interaction with them, correcting 'excuses' to what the actual workers involved might call them, 'perfectly rational reasons'.

I think direct address to the whole audience is rare just because it is so hard to imagine it. Here Heather Armstrong has been playing with a Flickr video she has made, one of many in which people read out words to show differences in accents (Coco is a dog).

> Watch Coco get so fed up with my Southern accent that she CAN-NOT TAKE IT ANYMORE and jumps off the couch. Welcome to our home, **Internet**, please remove your pants before stepping through the doorway. (*Dooce*)

The comedy comes from addressing 'Internet', the millions of people who might come across one's blog, the way one addresses a single visitor to one's house; in case we miss that this is comical, the usual 'remove your shoes' is changed to 'remove your pants' (US *pants* that is, not UK *pants*), perhaps to fit with the extreme informality of the imagined blog household of *Dooce*. As she shows, one can't address the real audience of a blog directly, because 'Welcome, Internet' sounds decidedly odd, a clash of the intimate and global.

6.3 Pronouns

Genres that try to persuade, such as advertisements, political speeches and junk mail letters, use a lot of *you*. Like *we* (see Chapter 4), *you* can have different meanings. It can refer to all the readers of the blog, at once.

> I wanted to share this story with **you** not only because a new recipe came out of the experience, but also because it was an example of how being limited can force you out of typical cooking routines, and help spark creative discoveries. (*101 Cookbooks*)

> What do **you guys** think? Can **we** raise that much? (*Bitch PhD*)

As we see in the *Bitch PhD* example, the use of you may draw the audience together, getting them to see themselves as part of a *we* (as readers of *Sepia Mutiny* refer to themselves as 'Mutineers'). It can also be used to a large or small group within the readership, or even to one person:

> And for **you traditionalists** who are worried about the coconut milk flavor – it isn't at all pronounced. (*101 Cookbooks*)

> Anyway, if **you** ever desire to bump into Malaika and Kamal, **you** know where to go. But please don't write about it! (*India Uncut*)

The latter example refers to an article about some celebrities seen (or maybe not seen) at a night club in Mumbai. So the *you* here is an imagined person (probably not a reader of this blog) who seriously cares about them. In contrast, *you* below, from the same blogger, seems to pick out a specific known person or persons.

> As much as I am embarrassed to tell people that I want to be an author because it has become such a clichéd ambition, I am also shamed by the fact that most of my close friends are genuinely talented writers, who work with far more rigor and discipline than I have been able to muster so far. (**You** know who **you** are, and I won't embarrass **you** with links.) (*India Uncut*)

Here Amit Varma is using the indefiniteness of *you* for rhetorical purposes; any of his friends can believe they are among the 'genuinely talented writers' referred to. Apart from these general, specific and very specific uses, *you* can also be a generic pronoun, meaning 'anyone'. Here Annie Mole has gone to the reopened London Transport Museum.

> **You** can lounge around on Northern Line upholstered seats and sip the tantalisingly named <u>The Anorak</u> & <u>Metropolitan Mixture</u> drinks. One can only guess what delights they might hold. (*Going Underground*)

The fact that *you* changes to *one* in the next sentence suggests that it is meant to set up a hypothetical situation in which a reader who goes to the museum can do these things. This generic use of *you* is common where people are talking about norms of behaviour or common practices.

6.4 Referring to the audience

A pronoun is one way of referring to or addressing the readers of the blog (that is, talking about them or talking to them), but of course one can do this in other ways as well. As with *you*, the reference can be to all readers, a specific set, or even to just one person. Here is *Dooce* reporting a conversation with her husband in which he suggested he was the 'coolest' spouse among those of her siblings.

> I was going to suggest a different adjective, but because I want to write about this conversation **on my family-friendly website** I'M NOT GOING TO. (*Dooce*)

So even as she talks to one audience, her husband, she imagines another audience for the written report in the future, an audience that will be offended by the use of this adjective. When Anna on *Sepia Mutiny* responds angrily to commenters who thought there was an inconsistency between her celebrating a traditional Kerelan (Malayalee) holiday and her being a Christian, she characterizes the audience she had imagined as she wrote, and also characterizes the smaller set of people who emailed her with responses:

> You know what? I wanted to put up something sweet, **for both the Malayalee readers and lurkers as well as those who may be interested in what Onam is about**, since to me, that is the best aspect of SM – the opportunity to teach and learn, express and listen.
> I did not write this so that I could get interrogated about my personal life or my beliefs. I have received emails asking me about my hypocrisy in celebrating Onam, since I am 'such a devout Christian' and all. It's not right. I'm not saying that **everyone who emailed me** was rude, but it does feel like an intrustion or a bit of an attack and it's bullshit. (*Sepia Mutiny*)

'Everyone who emailed me' is a reference to the group of people. But by referring to them, Anna also indirectly addresses them, giving her response. Geoffrey Pullum jokingly defines a large subset of *Language Log* readers who are desperate to correct him on his comments about *according to* and *lurk*:

> Updates, November 21: just in case **you** thought I had overlooked the following points, let me assure **you** that I was aware of them, and **you** do not need to join **the swarms of people** who are flooding the mail servers with messages pointing them out to me. (*Language Log*)

The *you* is addressed to this subset of readers, and he then goes on to refer to 'swarms of people', a category to which 'you' will belong if you respond this way. The *West End Whingers* make a similar but rather complicated reference to messages they imagine they will receive from readers:

> ** Footnote for pedants: Yes, since this video was made they have changed the lyrics regarding Lotte Lenya's nationality. We hope you are happy with yourselves. (*West End Whingers*)

The lyrics of a 'Fascinating Aida' song have been changed. They make a mock-catty remark about the people who notice this change, and then characterize the people who care about the whole business as 'pedants'.

As with *you*, the reference to audience can pick out an individual or a small group:

> PPS: I guess this shall simultaneously address a question on ~~everybody's~~ three people's (family and cat included) mind: 'What is Dave up to and why don't we see much of him here lately'. (*Dr Dave*)

Dr Dave has been blogging about a neuroscience article he has been reading, and in his postscript he imagines a very small group of people among his readership caring what he is doing. Heather Armstrong imagines the response of one person (and while she doesn't give the name, the underlined words are a link to her blog).

> And right about now a certain person who lives in San Francisco just regurgitated her lunch. She thinks there's only one opinion you can have about LA, the same opinion you might have about scrotal botfly infestation. That it is very unfortunate. (*Dooce*)

These references to the audience are rather uncommon, compared to the use of *you*, but they let us see various ways writers imagine, seriously or in jest, the multiple audiences they are addressing.

6.5 Questions and directives

Any utterance that isn't a statement assumes there is someone else there to respond; a question calls for an answer, and a directive calls for an action. Questions are a standard device in advertising for engaging audiences; however uninterested one might be, it is hard not to project oneself into the role of responding. Bloggers sometimes use questions and directives to elicit information or comments:

> What are your thoughts, do you think TfL have gone 'censorship mad' with Ann Summers? (*Going Underground*)

Laila El-Haddad in *Raising Yousuf* introduces a lighter note into her usually rather grim blog by posting some pictures of her son Yousuf and asking if his curly hair should be cut (that is, an afro or not an afro):

> Now a debate is raging in our household: Fro or no Fro? You be the judge! *(Raising Yousuf)*

Of course there can also be rhetorical questions, which you are not intended to answer:

> Does your dog do that? Hop on and off your bed, over and over again, because he is part Labrador, part douchebag? *(Dooce)*

Rhetorical questions work because they call on the reader to recognize a shared view or experience. Here the West End Whingers, writing about a play, set up an analogy and then make an unexpected use of it:

> You know how it is when you're caught up in a Hollywood action block-buster and then the love story kicks in and the characters start having sex and you find yourself looking at your watch? Well, imagine that but without the action block-buster bits. *(West End Whingers)*

This is funny (well, I think it is) because we first recognize in the question the experience they are describing, or at least recognize the sort of person who would find the movie sex boring, and then we are amused that sex could be treated as boring this way. And then the long question leads to a short directive.

Directives also suggest an audience by projecting someone out there who will do the action directed. Some of these directives are serious, in that the blogger hopes we will actually do what they say:

> Yes, **go sign up** now, but **come back here** to read the rest of the post when you're done. Thanks! *(Climb to the Stars)*

> ACADEMICS FOR THE SECOND AMENDMENT has been around for over ten years, but now there's a blog, and they're asking for donations to support an amicus brief to the Supreme Court in the D.C. gun ban case. I've supported them in the past, and I think they're a good outfit. **Note the PayPal button** at the upper right. *(Instapundit)*

The first directive is clear enough; she doesn't want to lose you while you check out the software she is talking about. The second example deals with constitutional protection for the right to bear arms. Note that it doesn't actually tell you to give them money; we are supposed to put together the fact that he has supported them, with the explicit directive to notice the button, to suggest that one might push that button to set up a way of donating (if one agrees with Glenn Reynolds' interpretation of the Second Amendment). Turn to the end of Chapter 3 for a particularly indirect directive.

83

Other directives are intended jokingly (even though the first one, about figs, says otherwise):

> But seriously, it's an underloved fruit – **do your part** to make them as popular as the[y] ought to be. I guess that's enough fig evangelization. . . . (comment to *Bitch PhD*)

> **Don't laugh too hard** at poor Miss Upton until you've successfully answered a few geography quiz questions under TV lights, that's what I'm saying. (*Language Log*)

The second example is meant to respond to criticism of a beauty contest participant who made a rather confused comment in a widely circulated video clip, but it also presupposes that we are, indeed, laughing at her. In neither case do we really have to do the action directed (promote figs, answer geography questions under TV lights); it is enough to imagine these actions, and draw the inference intended by the writer.

6.6 Enacting conversational interaction

In using questions and directives, the writer is interacting with the reader (see 'What I read' for more on this). There are other ways of suggesting interaction; one of them is to enact a bit of conversation, usually a rather odd one in which we, the readers, are projected as saying things we might not have said:

> The figs are all mine! **Mine, I tell you!** (*Bitch PhD*)

> **I know, I know**, you don't like purple. Or black. And that font over there is too small to read. And don't even get you started on squares, they're almost as bad as having to walk around with a rock in your shoe. (*Dooce*)

> **What's that you say?** You have no idea what I'm talking about? Fret not, almost no one ever does. The tale of Onam and Kerala's most beloved King is available for your edification, below. (*Sepia Mutiny*)

Of course readers may not be there in California to steal the figs from Bitch PhD; she is dramatizing a kind of childish tussle to show how much she desires the figs. In the second example, Heather Armstrong projects negative responses to her new web design on us, and then continues ('and don't even get you started on squares . . .') in rather elaborate free indirect speech, that is, it isn't presented as a direct quotation, but carries some of the style of how you would have said it. And Anna in *Sepia Mutiny* tells us, again in free indirect speech, what she imagines us, or someone, saying after reading the opening sentence of her post, and then comments jokingly that this is often a problem.

This kind of conversational self-interruption runs through a lot of blog style:

> And last but certainly not least, homemade bacon **(yes.. bacon bits!)** I love a strip of crispy bacon with many things I cook. Pancetta can be substituted of course. (comment to *101 Cookbooks*)

> So we've been eating lots of whole grains and fresh fish and green vegetables, trying our hardest to avoid foods with high fructose corn syrup, but do you have any idea how hard that is? They put high fructose corn syrup *in everything*, in ketchup, in pretzels, even in low-fat, baked potato chips, which I thought were legal, because **hello**, BAKED. That means 'not unlike God.' (*Dooce*)

> i received Christmas presents as a kid. I am a Hindu and agnostic **(shut up people**. I can be both like my Jewish secular friends, heh). (comment to *Sepia Mutiny*)

In each case, one needs to know a bit about the discussion to see why they have these interjections. In the first example, 'bacon bits' can be a commercial, artificially produced product, hardly appropriate for a foodie blog, but here, the commenter is making them himself or herself, and responds to an imagined objection. In the second, Heather Armstrong has an imagined, unstated objection, and then her voice responds with the name 'BAKED' (upper case signalling a shout). As if someone had asked what this means, she says they are 'not unlike God' again reported as if an authoritative voice from somewhere else. (They are not, unfortunately, low in the fructose that she is trying to keep from her kid.) And the commenter in the third example signals that he or she recognizes the oddity of saying 'Hindu and agnostic' by projecting readers who interrupt here, and responding rudely to them.

Conversational and paralinguistic features are so common in computer-mediated communication of all kinds that there are well-developed devices for suggesting them. There are, of course, the inevitable smileys:

> I agree that mainstream Zionists are not familiar enough with it, and thus many do not empathize enough with the pain of it. We have a lot to work on **(not much of a surprise, eh? ;))**. (*IsraeliMom*)

This is a very serious post, about the need for the two communities of Zionists and Palestinians to understand each others' narratives, but when she makes the criticism of her own community, 'we have a lot to work on', she projects a response to this, and her response to the response, and then she finishes with a wink smiley (which gets a bit lost in the parentheses). The same sort of move can be made with the kind of paralinguistic features used in roleplay games:

> Never thought of putting Home Fries (***wink***) in my soup! (*101 Cookbooks*)

The joke here is rather like the 'bacon bits' joke earlier; she has presented roasted potato bits as 'potato croutons' and the commenter is remarking that they are just the diner breakfast plate standard, home fries – but with a wink to show that the mocking comment is not meant seriously.

There is usually something self-mocking about enacting conversational devices in writing, because written texts are typically supposed to be whole and finished, and these devices suggest a constant self-monitoring and revision, in which one's own text is open for criticism or mockery. Here is an example from some witty theatre bloggers. They have gone on at length about the programmes, the drinks, the seats, the other critics there were the preview:

> So, yes, all in all a very agreeable evening.
> **Oh, and the play. Yes.** Actually quite good. (*West End Whingers*)

The joke, if I need to point it out, is meant to be self-mocking; as usual, they have gotten so wrapped up in the aspects of playgoing that critics usually ignore that they have apparently forgotten the part to which critics usually pay attention – evaluating the play. 'Oh' comes as a conversational response when someone has said something unexpected, here pointing out their omission. It is not conversation of course, but a rather sophisticated borrowing from some of the patterns of spoken interaction.

6.7 Implicature again

The items on my checklist are getting less and less direct in their engagement of an audience. In Chapter 3 I discussed Paul Grice's analysis of the way participants in conversation assume that the person with whom we are talking is trying to cooperate, to tell the truth, say as much as we needed to know, make it relevant to what we are talking about, and say it as clearly as possible. The main interest was in what happens when people flout these maxims, breaking them in a way that both sides realize they are being broken, so that the hearer (or reader) realizes that something more than what is literally said is being communicated. That further proposition or information is called an ***implicature***. Flouts happen all the time in conversation, and also in blogs. I will give examples of each of his four maxims. Let's start with an obvious one. Amit Varma is quoting President Bush talking about Pakistan, then giving his own comment:

[Pervez Musharraf] 'has been a loyal ally in fighting terrorists. He has also advanced democracy in Pakistan. He has said he will take off his uniform. He has said there will be elections. Today he released prisoners. And so far I have found him to be a man of his word.'

And in case the readers of this blog haven't figured out, **I'm Conan the Barbarian**. Anybody seen my battleaxe? (*India Uncut*)

Varma is flouting the maxim of quality (say what is true) because he is not, in fact, Conan the Barbarian, he is a mild-mannered Indian libertarian and cricket expert. We know that he intends for us to see that what he says is not true. We also see he is flouting the maxim of relation, because there is no obvious relevance of Conan the Barbarian to Pervez Musharraf. So we try to see what further propositions he may want to communicate that will make sense of this. One is that 'I'm Conan the Barbarian' is an obvious untruth, and so is Bush's 'He has also advanced democracy in Pakistan' and the other quoted statements. So why doesn't Varma just say this? Well, by saying it this way, he has shown us that we are already able to see the error of Bush's statement for ourselves; he is projecting a certain kind of audience response. (By the way, if Bush's original statements are false, that is not a flouting of the maxim of quality, but a simple violation: *he* does not intend for us to see these statements as obviously untrue.)

The maxim of quantity says that participants in conversation will normally say enough as is needed, and not more, for the purpose at hand. As we saw in Chapter 3, blogs regularly flout this maxim in the way they set up links:

UPDATE: Ouch: 'Aren't these the guys who are supposed to be keeping track of Iranian uranium enrichment?' (*Instapundit*)

The interjection 'ouch' suggests that somebody has been hurt by the remark in the link, but the remark itself is not enough to determine who or how. The missing information is supplied by the title of the link: 'un-weapons-inspectors-cant-even-count.html'.

Both the last two examples flout the maxim of relation; that is, it is not immediately obvious how one statement follows from another, and we are expected to draw implicatures that connect them. Amit Varma gives a good example of a flout of relation that by his admission doesn't come off, because readers were unable to come up with the implicature he intended. The original post is:

Dear Jeffrey Garten
Nalanda is in Bihar.
Regards
Amit Varma

The link takes you to a *New York Times* article by Jeffrey Garten encouraging the redevelopment of an ancient university in Nalanda. If Varma is following the maxim of relation, the most likely relevance is that this statement corrects something in the article. Apparently other readers had the same problem, because there was soon an 'update':

> I would normally never bother to actually explain a quip, but at least 15 readers have written in assuming that I implied in this post that Garten said that Nalanda is not in Bihar. Nothing of the sort. I was simply making the point that Nalanda happens to be in a state where the rule of law is absent, and therefore it is strange to think of building a world-class university there. I wasn't clear enough, I guess, so mea culpa! (*India Uncut*)

The problem was not, in fact, that Mr Varma was unclear; he just assumed he shared with his audience two further propositions that bridge the two statements:

> Nalanda should be funded as a world-class university (Garten in the *Times*)
> Nalanda is in Bihar (Varma in *India Uncut*)
> **A world class university cannot exist where the rule of law is absent (assumed)**
> **The rule of law is absent in Bihar (assumed)**
> Therefore 'it is strange to think of building a world-class university there'. (the update)

Why risk the misreading such indirectness allows? If readers who are more familiar with Bihar than I am (or Professor Garten, apparently) could supply these two statements, this witty way of putting his point would have also shown that the incompatibility of Bihar with a world-class university was already common knowledge, something that did not need to be said. But it did.

The maxim of manner just says that statements should be made clearly, briefly and in an orderly manner. Many blogs flout this maxim for witty effects, often mimicking or referring to other genres and styles (I think almost every example I give from the *West End Whingers* in this book is more elaborate than is strictly necessary to convey their propositional content). But here is a simple example:

> We also hoped that the change would help us go longer periods without getting sick. Maybe it all boils down to living with a ~~petri dish~~ **toddler**, but Jon and I have almost spent more time in the last year being sick than being healthy, and is it ever getting old. (*Dooce*)

Striking through 'petri dish' is not the simplest and most direct way of saying this, but it enables us to imagine that Heather Armstrong thought first of her lovely 3-year-old daughter as a laboratory container for promoting the growth of micro-organisms, before she corrected herself and recalled she is a toddler. So the elaborateness of the statement on the screen carries further implicatures about her (fictional) process of thought. It also projects an audience of readers who can sympathize with parents of toddlers, perhaps from their own experiences, and who can thus supply the unstated implicatures.

6.8 Politeness

Given the reputation of bloggers and commenters for casual rudeness, one might be surprised how commonly they go out of their way to signal politeness. By **politeness** here I mean the linguistic devices that can be used to soften any threats to the way another person might want to see themselves or might want to act (again there is a large literature on linguistic politeness; see 'What I read'). These threats arise all the time in blogs, for instance whenever one criticizes, directs or disagrees. Here is a simple example:

> At the same time, I think Palestinians, those living inside of Israel, those living in the territories, and just anyone who right now is anti-Zionists, should **maybe** take the time to open their own minds and hearts too to the Zionist narrative. (*IsraeliMom*)

This is a directive, and a serious one, not like the joking ones I discussed in an earlier section. But for 'anyone who right now is anti-Zionists', it is a considerable threat to *face* to accept an Israeli, of all people, telling them this, and implying them that they have had closed minds and hearts. *IsraeliMom* does not necessarily mean the *maybe* to indicate doubt; she clearly believes they must do this, as she must open her mind to Palestinian narratives. But such a weakening of a statement is conventional if one wants to soften a face threatening act. It may not make her opponents any more receptive to her point, but it does demonstrate to them, and to other readers who are neither Zionist nor anti-Zionist, that she is approaching them with a kind of respect. In a much less emotion-laden example, a commenter implicitly criticizes Heidi Samson for putting certain flowers in her picture of potato croutons:

> The flowers you used are beautiful, but you **might want to** be more specific about which versions are edible and where to get them. **I've always heard** the common garden varieties of marigolds are poisonous (and supposedly good for getting rid of some insect pests – mosquitoes? can't remember). (*101 Cookbooks*)

The bit of doubt at the end also works as politeness towards the blogger who provided the recipe, by denying any suggestion that the commenter is asserting their own botanical authority.

Such devices can also be used where the reader might see their free-dom of action restricted, in however trivial a way. Here Laila El-Haddad is merely asking readers to look up an old speech by a politician who has just died:

> **If you have a moment**, it **may** be worth **glancing at** Dr. 'Abd al-Shafi's <u>famous speech</u> from the Madrid talks. (*Raising Yousuf*)

This suggestion is offered with an adverbial opening and a ***hedge*** and a minimization of the action (*glancing at* rather than, say, *studying*), leav-ing you free to so as you wish. When Bitch PhD (whose name might not lead you to expect careful manners) gives advice to someone who has posted a parenting dilemma on her blog, she does it in the form of a question, interrupted by a criticism of her own advice:

> Skywind, **what about** simply presenting it to your son by saying 'some people think it's wrong, some people think that love is always a good thing' (**okay, admittedly** that's kind of a loaded explanation, but I wanted to avoid the 'wrong/merely okay' juxtaposition, which is loaded in the other direction) kind of approach? (*Bitch PhD*)

While there is all this politeness, there can also be deliberate impolite-ness. Rather than bore you with a lot of flaming (which also carries with it assumptions about the audience, just as politeness does), I will present a rather elaborate and witty example that also makes a point relevant to this book. Geoffrey Pullum wants to criticize the common assumption in his own field (and mine) that language is used only to convey information.

> **I'm sorry, I don't want to sound cynical and jaded**, but language is not for informing. Language is for accusing, adumbrating, attack-ing, attracting, blustering, bossing, bullying, burbling, challenging, concealing, confusing, deceiving, defending, defocusing, deluding, denying, detracting, discomfiting, discouraging, dissembling, dis-tracting, embarassing, embellishing, encouraging, enticing, evading, flattering, hinting, humiliating, insulting, interrogating, intimidat-ing, inveigling, muddling, musing, needling, obfuscating, obscur-ing, persuading, protecting, rebutting, retorting, ridiculing, scaring, seducing, stroking, wondering, . . . Oh, you **fools** who think lan-guages are vehicles for permitting a person who is aware of some fact to convey it clearly and accurately to some other person. **You simply have no idea**. (*Language Log*)

Pullum starts with signs of politeness in confronting those who hold this view, a direct apology and a possible self-criticism. But then he exacerbates any offense he might cause, by giving an excessive list of all the possible things language does besides informing, then addressing his opponents as 'fools' and finally upgrading, rather softening, his criticism, with the adverb 'simply' and an extreme form of the statement. The audience is not necessarily the benighted 'you' who believe 'language is for informing', but a wider group of readers who might be persuaded to reject this view. If we find this witty, it is because we think such over-the-top mockery is potentially well-directed, called for by the smugness of his opponents, or amusing in its elaboration. It makes us an audience by drawing on our projected response.

6.9 Expectations and knowledge

These last concepts, of implicature and politeness, draw on shared knowledge between the writer and the audience. Of course this is an issue in any other writing; writers write about what they think will interest their audiences. But shared knowledge is especially a point in blogs, because the best blogs, unlike newspapers, advertisements or poems, are written for relatively narrow audiences. *Sepia Mutiny*, for instance, is written by and for people of South Asian origin (desis) living now in North America. They share interests, knowledge about movies and music, norms of behaviour, and a specialized vocabulary. Here a commenter is commenting on a previous comment about dating:

> 'for some vague unexplainable reason, i tend to do much better with the **dbd** grls. . . .'

> I do better with **DBD Mallus** of any religion, than **ABDs**. I've decided that I will only marry someone **fob**ulous. Yeah, I said it. But I'm going to marry one so I can totally do that.;) (*Sepia Mutiny*)

I am not a desi living in North America, so it took some time on Google to figure this out. I can now tell you that ABDs are 'American Born Desis' and thus DBDs are 'Desi Born Desis'. The phrase FOB (Fresh Off the Boat), used by many immigrant communities, is here made into 'fobulous'. And *mallu* is a colloquial term for someone from Kerala, the writer's home state. Of course the intended readers don't have to turn to Google to get this information, so there is a pleasure in shared knowledge. This may seem an extreme example, but all the blogs I studied are full of terms that are known only to people within a certain community, for instance *Language Log* (syntax, semantics and phonology), *Cosmic Variance* (astrophysics), *101 Cookbooks* (culinary ingredients), *West End Whingers* (the London stage) and *Instapundit* (conservative US politics). In a broadcast medium, this might be a limitation; in a *narrowcast* medium like even a popular blog, it reinforces the sense, for the right audience, that they have come to the right place.

It is not just shared knowledge that draws audiences and bloggers together, but shared evaluations as well. I would guess that most uses of FOB in past generations have been negative; by coining *fobulous*, Anna and others have revalued it. More subtly, to say one does better with DBD girls, as a piece of news, suggests that the usual expectation is that an ABD young man would do worse with them. It is the evaluations that trip up outsiders to a blog community. As someone who works every day and rides a bicycle, I had trouble interpreting the following post at first, when Mildred is comparing her winter home in Florida (described here) to her permanent home in Massachusetts:

> It only takes me about 10 minutes to get to the local library. They offer many interesting programs which are held in the **DAYTIME** and there is a **large parking lot**. (*Thoroughly Modern Millie*)

Clearly 'DAYTIME' (her upper case) has some importance to it. Only when I read on did I realize that, for her, it is much easier to go somewhere in the daytime, and easier if one doesn't have to park a long ways away and walk over uneven pavements. Other readers her age, with her troubles getting around, will take these evaluations for granted. Shared evaluations can be very hard for outsiders to access, for instance on the cooking blogs or the political blogs. In this extended discussion of changes in the classic London Underground map, what counts as good design is taken for granted:

> The 1996 map is full of **clumsy kinks** and other design nasties all over the place. Its a very clumsy map indeed. Every kink on a map disrupts the flow of the lines and adds **complexity** to the map. (*Going Underground*)

The key here, I think, is the word *complexity*, which can be positively evaluated, in comment on a film, a piece of music or a sociological theory, and negatively evaluated in comment on a government policy, or here, on a famously simple design (The commenter, Max Roberts, turns out to be a lecturer in cognitive psychology, as well as a tube map enthusiast, which may be a clue to his use of the word). I will come back to the issue of evaluation in Chapter 7; the key point here is that it is one of the more subtle ways of projecting who is and is not in one's audience.

6.10 Big and small audiences

Much of the work on audiences has to do with mass media, starting with theatre and later press, cinema, radio and TV audiences. In all these media, the flow is more or less one way, though an effective actor, columnist or newsreader is aware on some level of possible audience responses. And in all these media, a bigger audience is usually better – it means more influence, fame and money. Blogs are different; they positively encourage many-to-many rather than one-to-many interactions. Of course some blogs are read much more than others. (It may surprise you to hear that *Dooce*, with its intimate voice and everyday anecdotes, currently has one of the largest audience of the blogs cited in this book.) But blogs, unlike plays, newspapers, books or movies, can work perfectly well with very small audiences, because they don't need a lot of money and equipment to get them started. If the blog of your trip to Montenegro is read only by your immediate family or friends, that could be fine, especially if they respond to it and comment in their own blogs, and if you write it to sound like the travel pages of newspapers or the guidebooks, you will alienate even them. I have come across intense circles of blogging around anorexia (for it), grammatical correctness, baking of sourdough bread, and as we have seen, the London Underground map. Success for most bloggers is having an audience, of whatever size, of readers who are engaged and responsive. Or as Rebecca Blood puts it, 'It is better to have the right audience than a large audience' (2002b: 96).

The techniques of engagement described in this chapter do nothing to produce a *large* audience; for that you need to have people linking to you regularly, and including you on their blog rolls, and you need to come up near the top of various indices such as *Technorati*. But they do help to produce the *right* audience, or rather, to assure readers that they are in the right place, and that it might be completely reasonable to interact with this total stranger on the other side of the world, by commenting or linking or quoting. Broadcasters have been told since radio days that they should speak as if they are talking to one person, not the millions who might be out there listening. Blogs speak to a group, but a group that seems to know each other and share a lot already. One sinks into a blog as one sinks into the sofa in a friend's living room.

6.11 What I did

For this chapter, I used all the blogs, but focused mainly on the posts rather than the comments, since the addressed audience in the comments is usually the blogger or an earlier commenter. I started coding the more obvious indications of audience, such as naming of the addressees (which turned out to be very uncommon), *you*, and references to the audience. Then I coded implicature and politeness, but those are so common that I just picked a few examples, instead of trying to find them systematically through the whole corpus.

6.12 What I read

Audiences are one of the key topics in media studies; for introductions to this body of work see McQuail (1997), Abercrombie and Longhurst (1998), Alasuutari (1999), Schrøder et al. (2003) and Brooker and Jermyn (2003). For blog audiences in particular, see Blood (2002b: Chapters 4 and 5) and Shirky (2008: Chapter 4). Erving Goffman's chapter on 'Footing' is in *Forms of Talk* (1981); he also considers these issues in *Frame Analysis* (Goffman 1974). Overviews of interaction in writing can be found in Thompson and Thetela (1995) and Hoey (2001: Chapters 1 and 2). On the uses of *you*, see Mühlhäusler and Harré (1990), and also Fairclough (1989: 210) on what he calls 'synthetic personalisation'. For introductions to Paul Grice's Co-operative Principle, see Levinson (1983: Chapter 3) and Leech (1983); Grice's original lectures are also readable (Grice 1989). On politeness, the standard reference is Brown and Levinson (1987); Watts (2003) has more recent work and Culpeper (1996) discusses impoliteness.

7 Opinions: Where do I stand?

The chapter in a sentence: Bloggers are often surprisingly careful in how they present their opinions to an audience, using a range of markers that suggest how they are making this statement.

We expect most bloggers to give us their opinions: on the Iraq war, a new Indiana Jones movie, the cooking of asparagus, Dunkin Donuts coffee, the seats at the Old Vic theatre or space-time curvature. Nearly every sentence has some sort of evaluation, explicit or implied. Even a simple list of links, the most basic of blog forms, asserts some sense of personal preferences or interests. So why would they need to tell us, one way or another, that what they are doing is giving their own opinion? One reason is that blogs are not all just rants in which authors shout their opinions at some imagined public; most bloggers adjust the ways they express opinions to interact with the audience and convey the complexity, interest and novelty of the views they are expressing. Take this sentence in a comment by jeff (referring to astrophysicists' tendency to ignore the problem of defining 'now' as part of their theories of time):

> Personally, I think they may be making a big mistake, but I don't know how else they could proceed, objectively. (comment to *Cosmic Variance*)

Within all this careful packaging, there is an assertion that 'they are making a mistake'. But there is a modal (**may** be making a mistake); the assertion is the complement of a main clause that says 'I **think** they may . . .', and that main clause is prefaced by an adverbial marking it as just jeff's opinion: '**personally**'. Then after the assertion, there is a concession, saying that jeff doesn't have an alternative.

These devices, taken together, are aspects, of *stance*, 'lexical and grammatical expression of attitudes, feelings, judgments, or commitment concerning the propositional content of a message' (Biber and Finegan 1989). Of course there are other markers in the example, including obviously evaluative words ('mistake') and words that may be implicitly evaluative for some writers and readers ('objectively'). But I will focus in this chapter on markers that separate out what Biber and Finegan call the 'propositional content' and make comment on how the writer relates to that proposition, for instance by saying 'I think'. These markers are part of a larger interactive process of *stance-taking* in interaction; here, jeff's interaction with Doug (who made the comment to which jeff is responding) and the larger audience of astrophysicists and other readers of *Cosmic Variance*.

Why should we pay attention to all this, and not just edit out all the verbiage and say that jeff says physicists are wrong? Well, for one thing, there are lots of these markers in blogs. And they do something: the passage from which this was taken would read very oddly if it had no stance makers at all. If it was just asserted, it could sound bullying and egotistical (and some blogs do indeed sound that way). Stance leads us to a more complex view of writers' opinions as more or less, certain or tentative, personal or collective. Attention to stance also leads us to a more complex view of how bloggers interact with potential readers, insisting they have something new to say, while also maintaining (usually) enough politeness to allow the discussion to continue, and to keep the blog entertaining.

The term **stance** covers features that are often discussed in other terms: modal verbs (*can, may*), some main verbs (*claim, think*), hedges (*possibly*), reported speech (*they say*), and conversational particles (*well*). I will consider the different kinds of stance-taking, and then divide the stance markers into those that use grammatical and lexical resources (such as adverbials) and those that use discourse resources (such as reported speech). In each category, I will go from features that are pretty obviously and commonly markers of stance, to constructions that are more novel and surprising, and that may stretch our conception of stance-taking. We will see that bloggers are quite careful about the ways they mark their opinions as (just) opinions.

7.1 Kinds of stance

Stance-taking can do different kinds of work; that is why it is an interesting concept. One of the big reference grammars of English, Biber et al. (1999), divides stance into three categories, epistemic (dealing with facts), attitudinal (dealing with personal perspectives) and stylistic (dealing with the way it is said). I was originally looking just for epistemic uses (which I cover in Chapter 8), and I find this categorization useful in pushing me to look at a broader range of stance-taking that is found in blogs. The next three sections deal with the differences between these kinds of stance before I look at attitudinal and stylistic stance in more detail.

i. Epistemic

Epistemology is the branch of philosophy studying how we know what we know. But we all deal with epistemological issues in our everyday lives, and epistemic stance concerns the marking certainty and uncertainty about the factual basis for statements. 'Facts are not our forte' is the wonderful motto of the *West End Whingers*, and it might serve as a motto for the entire blogosphere. The blogs I studied make surprisingly few statements of facts. But when the facts are uncertain, bloggers are generally rather careful in marking the uncertainty. For instance, *Instapundit* refers to some news reports, but raises doubts about them:

> ARE SOLDIERS **REALLY** BEING ASSAULTED <u>ON THE D.C.</u> <u>METRO?</u> Bob Owens looks into it and **it seems** to be mostly bureaucratic smoke-blowing – or ass-covering – based on a single incident. (*Instapundit*)

The author of *Instapundit* has very little direct access to news stories, sitting at his desk in Knoxville, Tennessee, and most of the work of his blog is in linking to various suggestions on the internet, and sorting out what he thinks can be believed from what can't. Here, he puts what might be a headline ('Soldiers are assaulted') as a question, and then puts an alternative interpretation in a report from someone else, and in a phrase introduced with 'it seems', which gives a carefully graded stance on this new view. If it turned out it wasn't mostly bureaucratic smoke-blowing, he wouldn't have misled you; he just said it *seemed* that way from what Bob Owens found, and it could well look different in the future, or even later that same day.

Unlike *Instapundit*, the author of *Thoroughly Modern Millie* has immediate access to what she is talking about here, the Passover practices of residents of her Florida retirement community.

> **I would say that** most of the population in this area either eat out or order a complete dinner and have it at home. (*Thoroughly Modern Millie*)

But she still marks it as just her perspective, by making her point the complement of a clause 'I would say that', leaving open the slight possibility that in some corner of the town she doesn't know about, a lot of Jewish residents are preparing chicken soup and matzoh balls entirely made from scratch.

Epistemic markers are relatively infrequent (compared to the other categories of stance), but they are very important, because they affect the way blogs are interpreted as part of news and political discussion (see Chapter 8).

ii. Attitudinal

The vast majority of instances of stance that I coded marked the writer's personal aesthetic preference, moral judgement or emotional response. Nearly every example later in the chapter fits in this category, so I will just give a few here, to show how much is covered by 'attitude'. Food bloggers frequently make statements that have no better support than the writer's own taste:

> **I humbly suggest that** the key to a good springtime curry is to keep things on the light side. (*101 Cookbooks*)

If this appeared without the words in bold, we would still know that this was just the *aesthetic* preference of Heidi Swanson (as she has other preferences for the less familiar grains, fresh vegetables and exotic salts). By emphasizing that it is just her suggestion, she actually strengthens it. Readers go to the blog just because they think her taste is pretty good, or is at least interesting, not because she claims any credentials to lay down the law on the authenticity of south Asian cuisine. The same sorts of statements might be made in blogs devoted to theatre, music, fashion or film, and often attention is drawn to the element of personal taste, as it is here.

Some attitudes are *judgements* based on moral or political norms, presumably shared with right-thinking readers. Here Angellos Makis, commenting on a post, presents himself as a Greek:

> **I am personally ashamed that** my country did not speak up of the Olympics been held in China. (comment to *Dr Dave*)

In this framing, the attitude is not just a matter of personal taste; he feels 'ashamed', implying that others will share his sense that Greece must be guardian of the moral and political norms of the Olympic movement, and that others will identify him as a Greek with the decision (or lack of decision) of the Greek government. Others make similar sorts of statements about parenthood, human rights, history or environmental action, implying that the issue is one that can be treated in terms of right and wrong.

Some markers of attitudinal stance convey an emotional response, rather than an aesthetic preference or a moral norm. Here *IsraeliMom* is talking about reading other blogs that in her view question the right of Israel to exist:

> **I confess,** these posts/comments upset me. (*IsraeliMom*)

She conveys her feelings, but frames the statement with 'I confess', implying that there is something secret about these feelings, or difficult about revealing them (even though we are hardly likely to be surprised

98

that they had this effect on her). Of course there is a moral comment here too; she is implying that the posters and commenters were wrong to threaten her country and her family. But in this sentence she conveys that judgement by talking about *affect*, about her feelings, rather than about right and wrong.

The three categories of aesthetic appreciation, moral judgement and emotional affect are useful in pushing us to look at the diversity of statements about attitudes, but like many category systems in this book, they soon get blurred. An affective response can lead us to a moral judgement (as we saw with the example from *IsraeliMom*). Similarly, a reviewer of a play who said it made her uncomfortable might use this affective response as a preface to favourable or unfavourable aesthetic stance-taking.

iii. Stylistic

When Heidi Swanson says 'I **humbly** suggest . . .' she is not just embedding the comment that follows, she is telling us how it is offered. In speech, much of the work of suggesting tone of voice can be done with intonation, volume and pace. In written genres, such as blogs, it may be marked explicitly. One device that has been much commented on is the smiley, such as :-) or ;-) or :^), all of which are used by various posters and (more often) by commenters on the posts, often to soften what could otherwise seem to be a harsh comment on someone else, or to mark an ironic or self-mocking comment directed at oneself or one's family. Here a blogger is writing about her annual move from Massachusetts to Florida:

> I know from experience the first few days It takes time to find the light switches, the cabinets where I keep the dishes, glasses, pots and pans. Not that I'm going to cook anything. ☺ (*Thoroughly Modern Millie*)

She scatters lots of smileys through her post, consistent with the light bantering tone.

Many examples of stylistic stance markers, especially adverbs (*seriously, honestly, frankly*) seem intended to mark a shift in tone, and not, perhaps, to describe the actual tone intended as serious or honest or frank. Let's take three examples, all from *India Uncut*. Here Amit Varma is suggesting that makers of a stuffed pastry put tandoori chicken in it to boost sales in the Punjab:

> **Seriously**, they should try it. (*India Uncut*)

I don't know about pavs, the pastry he is discussing, or about the Punjab, but I suspect this adverb signals that he is anything but serious in this suggestion. Another comment is about an ad for a vegetarian organization featuring a model wearing a lettuce bikini, saying (in Kannada) 'Turn over a new leaf':

> **Honestly**, in these circumstances that would be difficult even for a vegetarian, no? (*India Uncut*)

He does not mean that his previous comments were not honest, but more likely that we are now to read the literal meaning of the ad's slogan, and picture ourselves as males trying to turn over one of these strategically placed leaves (and presumably getting hit). In the next example, the marker of stance (unusually) follows the statement:

> To me, the Marvel superheroes just had more complexity – even more humanity, **if I may put it like that**. (*India Uncut*)

This metacomment draws attention, as a sort of afterthought, to the oddity of talking about the 'humanity' of comic superheroes who are, by definition, not entirely human. In fact, a stylistic stance marker seldom means exactly what it says:

> **With all due respect**, this sounds like a crippling way to learn an Asian language (i.e. a character-based language). (*Language Log*)

When one reads this phrase at the beginning of a sentence, one suspects that something potentially disrespectful (here, an unmitigated harsh evaluation of a proposed teaching method) will follow. When one is really respectful, such prefaces are unnecessary.

7.2 The grammar of stance-taking

So far I have been discussing the broad categories of functions of stance-taking. I will now take the attitudinal and stylistic categories and look more closely at the form of stance-taking devices. The categories are arranged to go from the more obvious marking of stance (a proposition in one clause and a statement of a relation to it in another clause) to less obvious means, such as adverbials and nouns.

i. Verb plus clause complement

In my data, by far the most common way of marking stance was to make the proposition the complement of a clause of thinking, speaking or wishing. A common verb in my data, and probably the prototypical verb for this purpose, is *think*. All three of the following are comments after posts that implicitly invited other opinions.

> **I think** this is a beautiful story. (comment to *Bitch PhD*)

> But **I think** everyone learns differently. (comment to *Language Log*)

> **I think** you should water your garden. (comment to *Raising Yousuf*)

Apparently the sentences would say the same thing if the first clause was left out; it is obvious that what they say is, usually, what they think. But in each of these cases, the writer is marking her or his statement as just her or his opinion, in the face of possible disagreement from other people. The first one is commenting on reports of a Chinese soldier breast-feeding survivors of the 2008 earthquake; by marking it this way, she suggests other people might not find it beautiful. The second example is responding to the assertion of a right way to teach Chinese; by marking it this way, he suggests possible opposition to earlier suggestions. In the third example, the blogger had said she wouldn't water her plant in North Carolina, in solidarity with suffering people in Gaza; by using 'I think', the commenter is marking her comment as a suggestion rather than as a directive. Some of the blogs and posts are peppered with 'I think', but only where the writers see themselves as being engaged in an argument.

If we take 'I think' as a neutral verb in the introductory clause, one can make it weaker by using a verb that does not carry the full force of *think*.

> **I wonder if** part of what I'm saying is that someone should have said to Parker, 'uh, are you sure you really want to go here?' (comment to *Bitch PhD*)

> And **I suppose** the EU laws on human rights add another layer. (comment to *BoingBoing*)

> **I guess** they'll need the cool dip after all the fire making efforts! (*IsraeliMom*)

> In fact **I rather suspect** there's a social continua of acrolect-mesolect-basilect for Mandarin and the other Chinese language-dialects in Singapore (paralleling the situation with English). (comment to *Language Log*)

> **It is my personal feeling** that the blogosphere has elements which may change us all, when we can indulge in peering into the souls of those affected by current events. (*IsraeliMom*)

Or one can embed the introductory clause (*I think*) in another introductory clause to weaken it still further. Here Heather Armstrong is talking about giving her father her new book, which has essays about fathers so it might be expected to have personal significance for him, and finding he has used it to straighten out his toilet.

> **I like to think** that I improved his life by those two inches. (*Dooce*)

She doesn't *think* this, she *likes to* think this, suggesting another viewer outside the speaking self who can see that this view (that she has improved his life) is a kind of wishful thinking.

Similarly, one can strengthen the stance by choice of verbs in the introductory clause:

> I **hope**, wait no, I **am sure** you'll have a good time in Tokyo! (comment to *Dr Dave*)

> I **truly believe** that in order to change things and arrive at a solid foundation for peace, we have to learn to accept each other narratives. (*IsraeliMom*)

Or one can present oneself as being compelled to say this, or as wanting to say the opposite, but finding themselves unable to:

> If 'sacrifice' is the yardstick by which we're measuring how American one is, **I have to say** that Amilcar is a hell of a lot more American than, say, I am. (*Bitch PhD*)

> <u>devin</u>: you know, **I wish I could say** this is intentional. (*Dr Dave*)

> **I must admit** i had slight teary sheen to my eyes after. (*BoingBoing*)

These constructions again suggest an adversarial situation in which the writer is positioning herself or himself against an opposing view, that she would have wished to say that he is more American than Amilcar, or he would have wished to say that this obscure writing by linguists is intentionally obscure, or that he didn't have tears in his eyes after watching a satellite landing on Mars. But he or she has to say it, so the statement is all the stronger.

The introductory clause doesn't have to be something like *think* or *say*; it can present a fact as relevant. Here the author of *Going Underground* is explaining with some embarrassment her occasional eating of fast food on the London tube:

> **It's just that** you're so limited for healthy food late at night near London Underground stations, you don't get much choice. (*Going Underground*)

Her behaviour is presented as following from this self-evident fact.

Conrad and Biber (2000) have suggested that the word order of these typical statements of stance is important: in nearly all cases, the readers get the stance in the main clause, before they find out what it is a stance *on* ('I think this is a beautiful story' has a different effect from 'This is a beautiful story, I think'). That makes sense, because it is important to know how to take a statement before processing it. An exception is the use of smileys, where one gets to the end of the sentence before finding that it is meant to display humour or shock, and abbreviations like LOL (laughing out loud) that give the effect on the writer after the statement. But they may act as a kind of insurance, in case you missed what should have been an obviously joking tone.

Let's consider one case of slightly odd word order:

> When I was a kid, eating poisonous toad excretions was the sort of thing **I never thought** you'd have to warn people not to do. (comment to *Boing Boing*)

In this phrasing, we get the 'eating poisonous toad secretions' first, and are allowed to figure out for ourselves that this is a stupid thing to do, so when the stance is given, 'I never thought you'd have to warn people not to', it comes as humorous understatement. At least I *think* that's why that comment is funny.

ii. Separate sentence

In the examples so far, the stance-taking clause (*I think*) comes first, and subordinates the clause that states the stance (*this is a beautiful story*). It should work the same way to have the stance-taking in a separate sentence. But it doesn't, especially if the stance comes after the statement. Here a blogger describes the approach to her local library in the evening:

> I remember going there last spring and found the street was not well lit, the sidewalk was irregular and there is no parking lot. That's not for me. (*Thoroughly Modern Millie*)

The first sentence is evaluative enough for us to guess her stance – she's not going there. But she makes it explicit, and also marks those elements as problems for her, not perhaps for everyone. The effect of putting the stance second can be one of an ironic turnaround:

> The Whingers are feeling a tad existential today. Not that they are *quite* sure what that means. (*West End Whingers*)

In the first sentence, the bloggers present themselves as people who can use philosophical terminology in this casual way, and in the second they undercut that self-presentation.

iii. Adverbial

An adverbial is a part of a sentence that gives an extra aspect of the meaning to the clause, saying how the action was done or giving circumstances:

> **Fortunately**, adding some common houseplants to your surroundings can apparently help clean up the toxins. (*BoingBoing*)

An adverbial can be one word, a phrase or a clause. It is the one part of a clause (subject, predicate, object, complement) that can easily be moved through the sentence (and trying to move it makes a good test if you aren't sure if it is an adverbial). So the following example could be rewritten with no difference in meaning:

> So which statistics do a good job of illustrating India's progress? One very good one, **in my view**, is the divorce rate. (*India Uncut*)

> **In my view**, one very good one is the divorce rate. (rewritten example)

> One very good one is the divorce rate, **in my view**. (rewritten example)

The difference is just stylistic, and I think we'll agree that Amit Varma got it right, using the adverbial for a pause before revealing his surprising choice of statistic. Adverbials can be used to qualify or support a statement by giving one's credentials, or to qualify it by saying it is just you:

> **As an Israeli civilian who has not served in the army** I say this without moralizing or judging. (comment to *Raising Yousuf*)

> **As far as I'm concerned**, the performers and director have made a pact with you, the audience member, when you buy that seat for a show, and that pact is to *give you a good evening* [italics in original] – to entertain you. (comment to *West End Whingers*)

Adverbials can be used to give the background or circumstances of a statement, or to attribute it:

> I was so happy to find enormous piles of cherries and other stone fruits (peaches and apricots) at the farmer's market last weekend! **For some reason** I wasn't expecting them until at least June . . . (*101 Cookbooks*)

> **According to Bill O'Reilly**, I am using the Presidential campaign to engage in 'villainous pursuits' to promote a radical agenda. (*Black Prof*)

The 'for some reason' adds the information that she was wrong and that she isn't sure why she was wrong; the 'according to Bill O'Reilly' marks this as not the author's own view (see Chapter 8).

The most frequent use of adverbials in these blogs is to weaken or strengthen the statement:

> **Certainly**, there are going to be more rough days ahead – especially as a cornered Al Qaeda feels the need to demonstrate that it is still a major force. (*Instapundit*)

Cyber-terrorism, **perhaps**, to mark the 60th anniversary of the Nakba? (*Raising Yousuf*)

Apearantly they both are pretty good about Native American issues. (comment to *Bitch PhD*)

Despite appearances, this **really** is just the standard cosmology, not some fairy tale. (*Cosmic Variance*)

Obviously the term has gained more prominence in this election cycle because it's the first time that the choice made by superdelegates has mattered so much. (*Language Log*)

As we have seen with other adverbials in discussing stylistic functions, the uses have often become conventionalized so that the words serve as markers and no longer have their literal meanings. 'In fact', for instance, seldom has the epistemic function of saying something is a fact (see Chapter 8).

iv. Modal and semi-modal verbs

Modal verbs come before the main verb and modify its effect:

I **might** ignore that 'makes about 48 petite bites' part and cut this sucker into pie slices. (comment to *101 Cookbooks*)

Terror? If there were giant poisonous hallucinogenic toads roaming the streets then that **might** warrant the use of 'terror' in the headline. Idiot ingests toxin and dies does not. (comment to *BoingBoing*)

The 'might' makes the 'ignore' or the 'warrant the use' only a possibility. They mark stance because they comment on the statement being made, although in a more subtle way than an introductory clause (The commenter could have said 'It is possible that I will ignore . . .'). Modal verbs are usually classified as *epistemic* (e.g., *may, might*, having to do with certainty or uncertainty), *deontic* (e.g., *should, must*, having to do with obligation or necessity) and *dynamic* (e.g., *can*, having to do with ability or inability).

Epistemic: Tomorrow **may** have a slightly higher entropy than today, but not by an amount that explains the radical difference in the behavior of memory over the two intervals (comment to *Cosmic Variance*)

Deontic: Black people **should** remain focused and be ourselves without worrying about what other people have to say. (comment to *Black Prof*)

Dynamic: Health officials said the hardened resin, made with venom from toads of the Bufo genus, contains chemicals that **can** disrupt heart rhythms. (*BoingBoing*)

105

As one might expect, blogs and their comments have a lot of the deontic category, people telling others what should happen or what has to happen. Modals can also be used to create a hypothetical situation that is contrary to fact. Here Heather Armstrong has told a cab driver that she writes a blog:

> I **could** have said, 'I teach English to genius pandas,' and the look on my face **would** have been the same. (*Dooce*)

She didn't say this, but she wants us to imagine the situation.

Besides the short list of actual modal verbs, there are also semi-modals that work in similar ways, for instance to express obligation:

> It took me a long time to even get into bulgur . . . I **need to** expand my horizons! (comment to *101 Cookbooks*)

> This morning, though, I **had to** check in at my neighbourhood clinic and undergo a whole series of health exams. (*Dr Dave*)

> It's always a quiet sad day, with sad songs on the radio and nothing but Memorial programs on TV (not that I **dare** watch any of them – way too painful). (*Thoroughly Modern Millie*)

These also modify the main verb to suggest the writer's stance. For instance, Millie could have said 'not that I watch any of them', but saying 'not that I dare watch any of them' she conveys the stance of avoiding them out of sensitivity, not out of boredom or disinterest.

Modal verbs have equivalent adjectives (e.g., *possible*), adverbs (e.g., *possibility*) and nouns (e.g., *possibility*), but I will stick to the verbs because they are less likely to be noticed as markers of stance.

v. Premodifying adverb

The term *adverb* sounds like *adverbial*, but they are different: an **adverb** is a class of words that modify a verb, an adjective, or another adverb. They are usually single words (there is one exception in my examples), and they cannot float around the sentence as adverbials do. Bloggers often add adverbs in a way that emphasizes their attitude to a statement.

> I'm **so** making this! (comments to *101 Cookbooks*)

> And it **totally** made viewers think that if they watched the piece they'd come away with some sort of gooey film in-between their fingers. Or a cold sore. (*Dooce*)

> but I **absolutely** know one thing – if I desperately needed help, these women would help me, no strings attached. (*Bitch PhD*)

> I've always liked Howard, but isn't this **kind of** gratuitous? (*Instapundit*)

In these examples, 'so' has to go before 'making', 'totally' before 'making', 'absolutely' before 'know', and 'kind of' before 'gratuitous', because those are the words they modify (*Kind of* is an example of a two-word adverb).

But their effect is more slippery and general than that precise word order would suggest. I still haven't figured out the use of *just*.

> **Just** one individual's thoughts. (comment to *101 Cookbooks*)

> I **just** chose to tell it from the point of view of a time coordinate that is oriented in the opposite direction from the one we usually use. (*Cosmic Variance*)

The *just* is always deletable, but it limits the effect of the noun phrase or verb, 'this and only this'. For instance 'just chose' means the same as 'chose', but the addition of the adverb stresses this is *all* he did; the implication is that a big difference arises from an apparently small choice. *Just* projects an assumed expectation onto the reader (it's only this), and then denies it (it's more).

Adverbs compress the kind of stance marker that we have seen earlier. The adverbs in the following sentence are the equivalent of 'I was disturbed that . . .' and 'We were irritated that . . .':

> Bourne delivers a superb performance, quite **disturbingly** convincing and – had it not been for the fact that Xavier's trousers were **irritatingly** too short for most of the play – Andrew would have been quite moved. (*West End Whingers*)

As adverbs rather than clauses with subjects, they suggest that anyone would be disturbed or irritated, because the explicit subject (*we*) is now implicit. There is the same effect from 'the fact that', which really means 'We thought that the trousers were too short'. Of course no reader will be confused by the lack of subject; in a theatre review, which is what the Whingers are writing here, everything is the writers' opinion. But there is a difference between marking the statement as opinion and projecting it, with adverb or noun, as already what everyone thinks.

vi. Stance nouns

I have been tracing stance markers from what I think are more obvious to less obvious grammatical forms. When the stance has been compacted into a noun (called **nominalization**), it may take some unpacking to see that it is the writer's opinion. Here Annie Mole is listing the advice she gave to bloggers at a workshop:

> The **importance** of primarily writing for yourself so that ideally your enthusiasm shows through. (*Going Underground*)

She could have said 'I think it is important that you write for yourself. . . .', but here that personal view is made into the noun *importance*, which makes it a topic one talks about, rather than an evaluation. A similar sort of compacting into a noun can happen with almost all the kinds of stance I have discussed. For instance, 'It is possible that there will be cheap shots' can be made into

> – but **the possibility** of this kind of cheap shot from media folks is one reason (among many) why I don't have them. (*Instapundit* [he's talking about blog comments])

At this stage, the explicit marking of stance with which we started has become rather attenuated, so the reader has to work to see it.

What's the point of figuring out the grammar of the stance marker? One reason is just to make yourself more aware of how many such markers there are in blogs. I didn't see how many deontic modals there were until I actually searched for them with a list. And it can be useful to note how they are distributed. There is one cautious comment in *Language Log* that uses 'I think' or 'I thought' seven times in a short paragraph. On the other hand, an angry post on *Raising Yousuf* asserting that Israeli actions in Gaza constitute genocide has no stance markers, except for a few deontic modals. Putting the stance marker in a separate clause or an adverbial makes it stand out, and signals the stance before the statement; putting it as a modal, adverb or noun makes it more taken for granted as part of the statement.

7.3 The discourse of stance-taking

i. Reported speech

The categories of stance-taking so far are tied to specific grammatical components of the clause. But there are also ways of suggesting the writer's stance by using structures that go beyond the clause, and rely on the reader's sense of how language is used in context. One way to do this is to use reported speech or thought to represent, often indirectly, one's own point of view. The examples that are relevant here dramatize a situation from which the reader can infer the writer's view. Since Heather Armstrong is particularly good at this, I will take all my examples from her blog *Dooce*. Nearly all her examples are hypothetical or modified reports that suggest what somebody would have said or could have said. Here she is describing how her father got her 4-year-old to eat pasta:

> I was all **YOU CANNOT BE SERIOUS, OUR DAUGHTER WILL NOT EVEN EAT BREAD**. And he was all, **woman, calm down, I am made of magic**, and after waving his hand and chanting a hypnotizing

spell, that kid put a noodle in her mouth, I WILL NEVER GET OVER IT. (*Dooce*)

Note that there is no reporting verb (*I said*, *he said*); the 'I was all' and 'he was all' suggest that she is giving more or less the effect of what was said, but not that these were her words. By dramatizing it this way, she takes a very ordinary everyday scene and conveys both her shock and her father's tone. In one bravura passage (about whether her work is to be classified as a 'mummy blog') she carries on a conversation first with herself, in reported thought, and then with her father, who is directly addressed:

> When I sit down to update my website I don't think to myself, **'What will I say today on my mommy blog?'** The first thing I think is, **how can I give my father a heart attack**? And then I back up a second and go, **nah, I'd miss him too much, I will just have to write this story about Jon's Brazilian wax in my personal diary**. Dad, are you paying attention? It's because of you that the world does not get to hear about Jon's genitals. I HOPE YOU'RE HAPPY. (*Dooce*)

The first, hypothetical report is given quotation marks. The second, 'real' thought is not given quotation marks, but is given in direct speech (that is, the tenses aren't shifted). The shifts to reported speech or thought are often seamless. Here she starts describing the studio of the NBC *Today* show, and then conveys her shock at the mess backstage with a sudden shift to direct speech:

> Not that I was expecting the walls to be lined with gold, but you look at the set and see how sharp and clean it is, and then you go backstage and, **oh my god, has my daughter been playing in here**? (*Dooce*)

Again, no reporting verb; readers have to be awake to the dramatization, as they would be in conversation, where such hypothetical reports are common.

ii. Rhetorical questions

We saw the use of questions in Chapter 6, as ways of engaging with the audience. Real questions may not convey stance; they may just be requests for information. But rhetorical questions, to which both writer and reader already know the answer, always convey a stance, if only by aligning writer and reader in this way. For instance, this question conveys a view of the plays of Bernard Shaw even if you don't know enough about them to share the evaluation:

> When did you last see the words 'Shaw' and 'concise' in the same sentence? (*West End Whingers*)

You now know that the Whingers don't think Shaw's plays are concise, and think their readers have already been bored by his characters going on too long. Generally, the reader's answer is known; in the following cases, the answer is 'No':

> Can you even imagine how one would go about envisioning the laws of physics spontaneously reversing a supernova, for instance? (*Cosmic Variance*)

> Maybe we shouldn't ever leave the house, otherwise? (*Dooce*)

> That is terrific, but do you think there'll ever be a time when a gay atheist has a shot at the presidency? (*India Uncut*)

The rhetorical question presents the point of view as obvious. Occasionally, though, the writer tells us the right answer, perhaps thinking we will miss it:

> If we are in the business of trying to understand, can we ignore a large part of recorded history because we don't like it. **I think not**. (comment to *IsraeliMom*)

iii. Irony

Irony, like a rhetorical question, attributes a view to the reader. Here, for instance, the reader must know these assertions are right (at least the date of the US Constitution), so putting it in a complement clause, using an adverb to weaken it, and then taking it all back, come across as ironic:

> I was *pretty* sure the nation was founded in 1789, that there was just the one candidate, and that there was no primary the first time around, but I guess I was wrong. (*Language Log*)

The effect is to suggest that the article he is criticizing has not just made mistakes, but has made obvious mistakes. There is usually some obvious contradiction to signal the irony:

> Albert Hofman, discoverer of the lysergic acid diethylamide compound (better known under its initials) and advocate of a mature, non-repressive approach to psychedelic drug experimentation, died this week at the age of 102. Yet another tragic example of a young life cut short by the evils of drugs. (*Dr Dave*)

Here the inconsistency of 'a young life' and 'the age of 102' makes us look for an alternative meaning, a mockery of warnings about drugs.

iv. Concessions

All the discursive markers of stance so far involve holding up some possible alternative view to one's own. The most obvious way to do this is to make a concession, usually stating some opposing view first:

> I think Nottingham University, and the police, and the home office, have acted appallingly in this case, **but** it isn't helpful to have this sort of grossly inaccurate reporting. (comment to *BoingBoing*)

> Yes, many events are documented, and I have a lot of respect for history as a discipline, **but** in the end of the day, we can go on arguing forever, because each side will pick the events that best suit their narrative, emphasize some events, and ignore or play down others. (*IsraeliMom*)

> The three instructions may be 'motherhood' (ie, obvious, although even that is arguable), **but** that property is not the same as being meaningless. (*Language Log*)

The adversative conjunction (but) signals the beginning of the view one holds and wants to emphasize. The construction shows that one has rationally considered alternative interpretations (of the case, the importance of history, the instructions discussed earlier), and then arrived at one's own view.

v. Conversational devices

Blogs have a surprising number of particles and non-word sounds that don't usually appear in writing, but that can be imagined in speech. They occur most frequently in response to some earlier post or comment. Here is a typical exchange, after Israeli Mom had moved to her own URL:

> ontheface said . . . So does the move mean that you're going to post more often? ;)
> IsraeliMom said . . .
>   **Yesssssss**! Well, **ummmm**, yes, I mean to post more often, we'll see what life has to say about it, I guess! (*IsraeliMom*)

She doesn't just say 'yes', she spells it in a way that suggests a high-pitched drawn-out conversational response. Then she gives an alternative, with 'well', a long-filled pause 'ummmm', and a plain 'yes', suggesting that her initial enthusiasm may need to be qualified. I found lots of different words and non-words, usually at the beginning of a negative response to some point or suggestion:

> **Harrumph** (*Bitch PhD*)

> I mean, **gee**. (*Bitch PhD*)

> **Um.** The intent of Memorial Day is to remember the dead. **Soooooo** . . . it's not the kind of thing of which you're meant to wish for happy observance. (comment to *BoingBoing*)

oh nooooooes (*BoingBoing*)

GEE, DO YOU THINK? John Kerry as an imperfect messenger. (*Instapundit*)

Sigh. Not much more to say. (*IsraeliMom*)

These do not just convey a response, they also set a joking tone, a shift from writing to mock conversation. We will see lots more of these in disagreements in *Wikipedia* (Chapter 9).

What all these discourse devices have in common is that they ask the reader to imagine an interaction, typically an adversarial interaction, and then draw inferences from the way the blogger is interacting. So they work differently from the grammatical markers; they can't be identified on their own, but have to be read for a specific meaning in context.

7.4 Why stance matters

Bloggers are often accused in the media of being solipsistic ranters shouting at an empty internet. It wouldn't surprise these accusers that I have found so many opinion statements in blogs. But it might surprise them to find that these opinions are so carefully marked, in many cases, for the way the writer holds them, the way he or she says them, and their basis of lack of basis in fact. One reason to look at the categories of stance-taking is to see the wide range of ways bloggers relate to what they say. Another reason to look at these categories is to see, again, how interactive blogs must be to survive. The blogs I have analysed vary in their numbers of readers, but they all do interact with their readers in nearly every sentence. The pleasure in reading something like *Dooce*, *Instapundit*, *India Uncut*, or *Going Underground* is not just in getting the opinions – I certainly don't agree with all of them. It is also in seeing how cleverly they manage that interaction and keep it going.

7.5 What I did

For this chapter, I took the blogs listed in Chapter 2, and analysed them using Atlas ti (see Chapter 10). I started with the grammatical categories from Biber et al. 1999, and added discourse categories to them. The categories of rhetorical questions and conversational devices, for instance, emerged as I went through the data. In general, there are far more markers in the readers' comments than in the bloggers' posts. As my choice of examples suggested, there are far more stance markers in some blogs than in others; I found relatively few in *Black Prof,* and huge numbers in *BoingBoing* and in the academic discussions on *Cosmic Variance*.

7.6 What I read

There is a large literature on stance. The chapter in the *Longman Grammar of Spoken and Written English* (Biber, Johansson, Leech, Conrad and Finegan 1999) can serve as a starting point, and several collections extend the concept from grammar to discourse and interaction (Hunston and Thompson 2000; Englebretson 2007). *Stance* is a rather broad umbrella term; there has been far more work on what I have treated as specific categories, such as modality (Palmer 1990; Fairclough 2003), hedging (Hyland 1998), reported speech (Semino and Short 2004) and narratives (Eggins and Slade 1997; Georgakopoulou 2007). Of course none of these studies refers specifically to blogs; you have to go back to studies of other genres of writing and speech.

8 Evidence: How do we know?

The chapter in a sentence: Bloggers can mark their statements of fact as based on induction, deduction, hearsay and belief, using many of the stance markers in Chapter 7, and they mark this evidence in relation to audience expectations.

In the last chapter, I considered ways bloggers mark their stances. Here I want to consider one specific and important area of stance: how they mark what they know and what evidence they have for what they believe. I have chosen examples mainly from the news, because that is a kind of writing in which facts particularly matter, and in which evidence for them is often challenged.

Let us start with one example of a blog and an event: bombs on the trains in Mumbai, India on 11 July 2006. If this had happened a hundred years ago, there would have been a report from a correspondent, probably not a long one, in each of the major British newspapers. It would have taken time for the correspondents (perhaps in New Delhi or Calcutta) to get any news, so even with telegraph the report might have appeared several days later. And since the events would have been so remote (even for a Britain with colonial interests in India), the reports might not have merited much space alongside domestic murders, party politics, royal events and cricket scores.

But since it happened in 2006, not a hundred years ago, there were reports within the hour, constantly updated, on CNN and the BBC, and on web pages of the *Guardian*, the *New York Times*, the *Times of India*, *Hindustan Times* and many other news organizations (there is a time-line of coverage at http://gauravsabnis.blogspot.com/2006/07/blasts-in-bombay.html). The television news network CNN-IBN actually had a correspondent on one of the trains. And there were the bloggers: Amit Varma, of *India Uncut*, had a post within hours linking to various news sources, and updated and corrected through the day. By the next day, he had also linked to many other blogs commenting on the events (*Instapundit*, *Sepia Mutiny*, *UltraBrown*), and new blogs and wikis allowing relatives and survivors to contact each other, and had posted his own comment on the *Guardian*'s *Comment is Free*, with many comments on that. I will come to some passages from these posts later in the chapter.

Blogs as news have all the reach and immediacy of satellite television, with all the unreliability of the web. Blogs provide first-hand information about places correspondents seldom reach, and access to people with an astonishing range of expertise, and they can send vivid pictures and videos within minutes of an event. But they also recirculate endlessly repeated statements with no basis in fact (as in this case, speculation about the motives of the bombers). So how do we as readers find our way in this sea of statements? We could and should do all the traditional procedures: checking on the source, checking who is quoting the source, looking for corroboration from a different source, evaluating evidence, testing assertions for consistency. In this chapter I consider how bloggers mark the evidence for their facts.

8.1 Evidentiality

I said in Chapter 7 that epistemic stance, dealing with how we know what we know, is a part of everyday life. Just yesterday I overheard on a train two men talking. 'Did you see him?' one was asking. 'You see this?' In many languages, speakers must mark statements to show what kind of evidence they have for them, for instance, adding a particle to show that what one is saying is hearsay, heard from someone else rather than seen for oneself. In English, of course, such marking is not required (that's why the man on the train had to check). But there are ways of marking evidence, or the lack of evidence, just as there are ways (as we saw in the last chapter) of marking other stances. Professionals who make facts their business – such as journalists, spies, medical doctors and academics – have developed elaborate codes for indicating how sure they are of a statement. Bloggers are less worried about such indications; they typically present themselves as part of a world of opinions, exclamations and gestures referring to apparent facts gleaned from somewhere else. But there are still traces of evidence, and they matter to careful readers.

As a starting point to understanding such qualifications, we can go back before the rich recent studies of stance and hedging to an earlier and more general overview by the linguist Wallace Chafe of the ways one can state a claim in English (Chafe 1986). Chafe presents four 'modes of knowing': induction (knowledge derived from particular cases), deduction (knowledge derived from general principles), hearsay (what others have said) and belief (what one just knows). I will review these categories in blogs, and then look at some of the ways they are communicated.

8.2 Induction

Blogs sometimes present themselves as tools for **induction**, reasoning from the specific to the general; bloggers say one just needs to read a lot of these accounts before arriving at a broader and more reliable view of the world.

> **I find that** if I keep the salad greens separate until just before serving, they don't go soggy. (*101 Cookbooks*)

This poster offers the statement as a general fact about salad greens, based on his particular experience. The reasoning may also be based on what one has seen, perhaps in mediated form.

> Sahhaf, the Minister of Information, would say, 'There are no tanks in Baghdad!' and yet, explosions and the carcasses of burnt up cars with families still inside, said otherwise. (*Baghdad Burning*)

The blogger is moving from pictures she saw of the 2003 US invasion (on Iranian television) to a conclusion about the situation that contradicts the assertions of the Iraqi Minister of Information. The induction often works this way, as the gathering of evidence that contradicts a view asserted elsewhere. In the following example, Amit Varma is sceptical about a newspaper report of prostitution at two coffee bars in Mumbai.

> 'these places were being used by pimps to solicit clients.' Odd. Those outlets are fairly close to my office, and used to be as close to my residence, and I go there often. (*India Uncut*)

Juxtaposing a quotation with the blogger's own experience is a common tactic in many blogs, because that is just what bloggers have to offer, a single point of data for us to combine with others, their job, their education, their reading, or their view out the window.

8.3 Deduction

While induction moves from specific cases to a conclusion, **deduction** involves reasoning from general truths to specific cases. One commenter on *BoingBoing* says,

> I know Cory is an Anglophile and thus tempted to insert 'u' into all sorts of strange words, but please, not Arabic transliterations.

No one defends the spelling of *Al-Qaeda* with a u in it, but another blogger responds by reasoning from what they assume to be the general principle that Canadians use British English spellings:

> Cory is Canadian. He **therefore** uses British spelling. Nothing to do with being an anglophile. (comment to *BoingBoing*)

This is a syllogism with one premise left to us: All Canadians use British spelling (not stated); Cory is a Canadian; therefore Cory uses British spelling. In *HeadHeeb*, the author assumes that a principle is so well established (within the UN) that it must be applied to this specific case (the status of Montenegro in relation to Serbia).

> Secession by consent is well enough established in international law that it [the UN] couldn't really refuse (*HeadHeeb*)

He is not saying that he believes the UN *should* approve the secession, but that to be consistent, it *must*. It is perhaps not surprising that the blogs I studied have few statements based on general principles; their job is the gathering in of scattered instances, and though they often generalize, they seldom reason logically from these generalizations. Where they do make big general statements, they are often joking, sending up the serious advice of more authoritative genres.

8.4 Hearsay

Hearsay is Chafe's category for evidence offered on the basis of language – someone else saying or writing something. We think of bloggers sitting at desks, eyes glued to computer displays, so at first it might seem that most blogs offered hearsay, by definition. Here is an example where the blogger on *Global Voices Online* is repeating what has been said by witnesses to the stealing of some tents meant for earthquake aid.

> **Some citizens said**, on 21st, afternoon, a middle-aged man played Mahjong with several women inside, when someone questioned where the tent was from. The man stated, he 'took the tent because of connection'. (*Global Voices Online*)

This is presented not on the blogger's own authority, but on the authority of 'some citizens' who wrote about it on their blog. Even apparently 'first-hand' reports like *India Uncut*'s reports from Mumbai, the reports in *Baghdad Burning* on Iraq, *Live from an Israeli Bunker* on the 2006 invasion of Lebanon, and *Raising Yousuf* on Gaza rely on rumours, news agencies and television, and all the other blogs on my list usually start with some link as an occasion for comment (see Chapter 3). The entry then establishes, sometimes obliquely, the writer's attitude towards the status of the source and the statement. This example concerns an incident involving a Baghdad shop that displayed the Brazilian flag during the World Cup.

> **According to the neighbor** Abu Rossul, the young cleric stopped, gazed at the flag, took note of the shop's name and location and went on his way. (*Baghdad Burning*)

'According to' separates the source from the quoting writer, suggesting she has evidence for this encounter. Her credibility is based on just such local knowledge.

On the other hand, mentions of sources can also mark a statement as less certain:

> **A tipster working for the IRS claims** on his blog that the IRS's archiving has been outsourced to the lowest bidder, an unnamed company in Florida. (*BoingBoing*)

'Claims on his blog' has a slightly different effect from 'according to', and the characterization of the source as a 'tipster' suggests that this tip is not necessarily to be relied upon. Here the cues of stance are rather direct; in other cases it can be harder to tell whether the author is affiliating with or disaffiliating from the quoted text.

> Not heard about this officially yet but the Inquirer report that '*The plan to enable mobile phones to work on London's underground railway network (aka The Tube) has been quietly shelved according to Martin Cassidy, president of Innovawireless.*' (*Going Underground*)

This is doubly hearsay, a newspaper (not an official statement) reporting one participant's view. As we will see later, such care in attribution means you can undo a statement of fact later, because it isn't you who made it.

8.5 Belief

Blogs are a genre that encourages the expression of personal views, so a lot of the statements are explicitly matters of belief, unsupported by any evidence. The source of induction is evidence, the source of deduction is hypotheses, the source of hearsay is language, but belief need not have any source at all, just an inner certainty. Here *Dooce* is talking about something in the future, the way her 4-year-old daughter will react when she grows up and reads what her mother is writing about her now:

> **I have no doubt** that you will spend years of your life resenting me and being embarrassed that we have the same last name, despite **the fact that** I have and will spend years of my life writing love letters to you on the Internet. (*Dooce*)

Future events are inherently uncertain (as every parent knows and fears), but Heather Armstrong actually heightens the certainty with which she asserts that she will continue to write, and that Leta will one day resent what she reads. The unrealistic certainty shows her commitment to this version of the future, and thus to her view that she is right to write about Leta in her blog.

Of course marking something as a 'belief' is not just saying that one has no evidence for it; it can mark a personal commitment to the statement. Here *IsraeliMom* is saying that the statement that follows is an important part of her way of thinking.

> **I truly believe** that in order to change things and arrive at a solid foundation for peace, we have to learn to accept each other narratives. (*IsraeliMom*)

The *have to* is the key here; she is invoking something she thinks is a matter of normative behaviour or judgement, norms shared with her readers. One could easily deny this statement (she wants Palestinians to respect the narrative Israelis tell themselves) but she is signalling that to do so would amount to an attack on her, and would make interaction with her difficult.

8.6 Verbal resources

Evidence is signalled linguistically by the same sort of stance devices we saw in Chapter 7, such as a cognitive verbs (such as *I think*) plus clause complements, modal verbs (such as *might*) and adverbials (such as *probably*). When these devices downgrade or upgrade the certainty of a statement, they are collectively known as **hedges**. Hedges may be used to leave open doubts about a statements.

> **If true**, it means that this company will control the most intimate details of the finances of **virtually** every American. (*BoingBoing*)

> **It seems** people who listen to a certain song by Himesh Reshammiya are being possessed by ghosts, and are emitting strange nasal sounds. No, I mean, really! (*India Uncut*)

The first sentence of the *India Uncut* report is presented as if a report, but the second sentence, with its exaggerated insistence ('No, I mean, really'), signals that Amit Varma thinks this is rubbish.

I looked for hedges in blogs, and found surprisingly few of them; where they are used, it is often for comic effect. Here, for instance, the author uses a hedge to point up in a comic way the hyperbole of the claim.

> Prior to the war, his wife and sister ran the shop, making the most persuasive sales duo in the history of cosmetics **probably**. (*Baghdad Burning*)

The blogger is weakening what is obviously a hyperbolic claim, that is, one exaggerated for comic effect. Why is there so little marking of epistemic caution in blogs? After all, many of their statements range from the speculative to the unlikely to the preposterous. But bloggers seem to operate in a realm of licensed gossip, according to a different standard of evidence from what one might find in academic articles or even newspapers. It could be (see, I'm doing it) that hedging is unnecessary because any statements in blogs are considered by default to be speculative and revisable. As we have seen (in Chapter 5), Amit Varma and others do revise their blogs, visibly, as the facts are revised. That turns out to be an excellent device for breaking news, but is a less effective way of qualifying rumours and suggestions, which, once uttered, can't be simply stricken through and forgotten.

One might think that one verbal resource for marking something as a fact would be to say that it is a fact. But the most common ways of doing this in English also has other functions. As one English grammar puts it, *in fact* 'not only shows actuality, but also connects the proposition to the preceding sentence, which it strengthens or makes more specific' (Biber et al. 1999).

> Enjoy the rest of your time in Florida and don't be discouraged – there's no more snow that I can see on the north shore – **in fact** it's gorgeous today. (comment to *Thoroughly Modern Millie*)

Here a commenter says first that there is no snow, and then a heightened version, 'it's gorgeous'. *In fact* can also be used between any two alternative phrasings:

> In their most recent report, the International Crisis Group found that 'The policy of isolating Hamas and Gaza is bankrupt' and has **in fact** backfired. (*Raising Yousuf*)

To say the policy has 'backfired' is worse than saying it is 'bankrupt'; it's not just that it didn't work, but it actually worked against the intentions of the policy-makers. So *in fact* does not mark facts, it marks this kind of upgrading.

The fact that also has a discourse function besides that of marking facts; it is one of the most common ways of packaging a clause so that it can function as a noun phrase.

> **The fact that** [they want you to have your ears showing in the picture] was a bit baffling, but the most surprising thing for me was that you're not allowed to smile for the picture . . . (*IsraeliMom*) (brackets added)

IsraeliMom is not insisting that the US requirements for a visa photo are facts; she is using this phrasing to take that whole clause (indicated by brackets) and make it a noun phrase that can be the subject of the sentence (it was baffling). The construction can make any clause (indicated again with brackets) into a noun phrase:

> And it was during this phone call with my friend that I remembered dating a guy in Los Angeles who was very refined and had a great sense of humor, and we got along in every way except for **the fact that** [he talked like a muppet during sex]. (*Dooce*)

Only Heather Armstrong and her unfortunate temporary boyfriend could tell if this was a *fact*; the point here is to make it something she can talk about, and that she can put at the end of the sentence, where it will have a comic effect in contrast to the earlier descriptions ('very refined', 'great sense of humor').

Readers have to be careful, though, because calling something a fact is often a way of asserting something that would not be seen as a fact by everyone:

> **The fact is** male lives are falling apart at the growing margins of male welfare, and the utter failure of the education system to address male needs on male terms is indeed a crisis. (quoted on *Instapundit*)

Thomas Mortenson (who is quoted here) says 'male lives are falling apart' as part of an argument that men are unfairly treated in relation to women in higher education. 'The fact is' just marks the contrast between his view and the views of those he calls 'feminists'; it doesn't make his assertion a fact. The phrase can also be used to mark statements that everyone agrees with, but that are not the issue. This is from a comment posted on *Global Voices Online* after earthquakes in Szechuan province:

> I believe that somehow, someway this may open the chinese goverment up to **the FACT that** we are all one race . . . the human race . . . and we need each other. (comment to *Global Voices Online*)

The capitalization, which is there in the original, suggests that the commenter thinks someone might disagree with the assertion, but 'we are all one race' is something with which most people agree, including the Chinese government; the issue is the relevance of this assertion to their policies on Tibet or civil liberties. So in general, when someone says something is a fact, you have to ask why they think it necessary to say so.

8.7 Evidence and interaction

Chafe suggests that the way one makes a statement of fact depends not only on one's evidence for it, but on the expectations of the writer and reader. As we saw in Chapter 6, blogs are designed for specific audiences with specific knowledge and limitations. Consider this comment as *Baghdad Burning* asserts that Iraqi celebration of the World Cup differs from that in other parts of the world:

> **Oh** we have flags and banners **too**. (*Baghdad Burning*)

The particle *oh* is conventionally a mark that this is news to the speaker. It is as if you the reader had said that you thought that Baghdad did not have World Cup hype, and now she is responding to your comment. This projects us as an audience outside Iraq, watching it on the television news, so we don't know. Other devices can be used to grant that we do already know, most often *of course*. Here a commenter returns to the issue of Cory Doctorow's misspelling of Al-Qaeda with a *u* in it:

> And **of course**, it's an extremely easy mistake to make, for exactly the reason you suggest. (comment to *BoingBoing*)

The rhetorical point of granting such expectations is to set up an assertion that might not be expected. Here astrophysicists are considering the testability of alternative cosmological scenarios, for instance one in which time goes backwards:

> Further testing is, **of course**, a really messy problem, but is in principle possible. (*Cosmic Variance*)

Even non-physicists reading about testing cosmologies will agree that is 'a really messy problem'; the commenter wants to take our attention off the practical difficulty to focus on the idea of its theoretical possibility.

This attribution of expectations can serve to build up our solidarity with the writer. Here Heather Armstrong is talking about a joke her father played, saying that he had used his baby-sitting time while Heather was on television to cut his daughter's hair.

> No, **of course** he hadn't cut my daughter's hair, he just wanted to jar my heart enough that it would compromise my immune system. (*Dooce*)

Now I am not in a world in which it is absolutely unthinkable that a grandfather might cut his granddaughter's hair and ruin the look her mother has carefully created (I might come to understand this if I become a grandfather). But the *of course* attributes that belief to me; he can't have done this because this would be beyond belief. A story of how a teacher saves her students projects on us the expectation that the students would have to be hurt when the school building collapsed on them.

> 'They are all alive, except the teacher.' When asked if they were hurt, **of course** they were, but the 4 surving students shook their

heads, because they were greatful to be saved by the teacher. (*Global Voices Online*)

With this structure, the stress can be placed on the students' brave denial of injury under the circumstances.

Of course is, then, a rather tricky construction. The expectations projected may not be those we actually have:

> **Completely contrary, of course, to our conventional expectations**, which are that (1) polarized waves maintain their polarization angles in empty space, rather than rotating, and (2) every direction in the sky is basically equivalent to every other direction. (*Cosmic Variance*)

If your knowledge of physics is like mine, you did not have the 'conventional' expectations in (1) about the behaviour of polarized waves, but you may well have had expectation (2) without thinking about it. *Cosmic Variance* politely attributes knowledge to us, but also tactfully restates it in case we'd somehow skipped physics class on the day polarization was covered. *HeadHeeb* makes a similarly polite assumption about our detailed knowledge of negotiations about an important (but then underreported) humanitarian crisis in Africa:

> **As most of you are no doubt aware**, talks in Ljubljana have failed to convince the two holdout factions to sign the Darfur peace agreement (*HeadHeeb*)

Many people were probably unaware at that point of the Ljubljana talks, or of the events at Darfur, but *HeadHeeb* attributes knowledge and concern to his readers. As we have seen in Chapter 6, such projections do not just respond to audience knowledge, they create an ideal audience as a community sharing certain kinds of knowledge, values and responses. Assumptions about audience expectations are why *Instapundit* can have this posting, which he seems to say is entirely predictable:

> **I CAN'T SAY I'M SURPRISED** BY THIS REPORT: . . . (*Instapundit*)

Well if he is not surprised, why should we click on this link, since news by definition has to be something of a surprise? He is assuming we know and share enough of his view of the world that we too see the story as a confirmation of this view, and for that reason will try to find out what the link says.

The projection of expectations in blogs relates to a wider issue that has been much discussed: the tendency of readers to stick to blogs that just confirm what they already expect. The danger of such a pattern, in which blogs project audiences and readers seek out sympathetic blogs,

123

is that we don't ask if a statement is right, we ask how it fits in with what we already know or believe. This circularity is not a problem when the issue is one of private preferences (blogs on operas, theatre, bread-making or football), but is more worrying with public issues (global warming and its consequences, the pursuit of the war in Iraq, the effects of gun control).

8.8 Undoing facts

One advantage often suggested for blogs over print news is that statements in blogs can be revised, as we saw in Chapter 5. The first report of the Mumbai blasts on Amit Varma's blog, *India Uncut*, marks the changed figures that came in over the course of an hour:

> At least ~~four~~ ~~six~~ seven* bomb blasts reported so far in Mumbai . . .

The crossing out doesn't just give the correct figure, it records the changing state of knowledge. The adverbial 'at least' starts the statement by conceding his knowledge is partial, the verb 'reported' presents this as a fact that he has only by hearsay. Later in the day, the statement is presented as fact, without any hedging:

> Seven bomb blasts have taken place across Mumbai, along the Western Line railway, at rush hour.

But he is more cautious about the details.

> The exact locations are *still* not being clearly reported (see conflicting versions here and here), but this map (via Counterterrorism Blog) seems to be roughly correct.

The reports of locations are not 'exact', they are not reported 'clearly', they are 'conflicting', and even those on the recommended blog are only 'roughly' correct. One gets the idea of Varma sorting rather carefully through the various versions. When bloggers have to take it back, they are not usually cancelling something they asserted themselves; they are cancelling something they thought, or heard, or concluded.

Some kinds of statements of facts can be taken back, while others can't. Here is a sentence, not from a blog but from Susan Sontag's diary for 19 February 1959:

> Also there was a man who looked like Jean-Paul Sartre, only uglier, with a limp, and was Jean-Paul Sartre. (*Guardian* 14/9/06)

Sontag did not say explicitly that the man wasn't Jean-Paul Sartre, but we assume that if she could have said she had seen him, she would have, so she has had to say something weaker, he just looked like Sartre.

That conclusion we arrive at indirectly (it's not Sartre) is an ***implicature*** (see Chapters 3 and 6), and implicatures can be cancelled. We don't think she is talking nonsense, we think she is trying to convey some other information, perhaps that Jean-Paul Sartre doesn't look entirely like what she imagined. The way implicatures can be cancelled like this is called ***defeasibility***.

Defeasibility is related to the wider issue of self-correction in blogs and other media. Of course newspapers have long had spaces devoted to correcting their errors; there is a website devoted to these corrections (http://www.regrettheerror.com/). Newspapers correct the next day, or later, often after a complaint, or a word from lawyers. Blogs would seem to have the advantage that they can correct immediately, in the same place as the error, and still show the error, for instance by putting strikethroughs on the now outdated or corrected text. The strike-through reminds us of the provisionality of facts, while the print of newspapers may suggest a definitive account. But I wonder if the provisionality accorded to facts in blogs has its own dangers. A statement can be quoted in other blogs, linked to, commented on, and even if it is taken back an hour after it was posted, it continues to circulate.

8.9 Blogs, evidence and news

Given all these markers of evidence, why do you believe (or not believe) what you read in a blog? Some commentators have seen the rise of blogs as part of a shift in the status of journalists and other professionals, and a welcome rise in the status of ordinary people. Over the twentieth century, journalism developed into a profession in the US and many other countries, with graduate training, professional organizations, and implicit but very strongly felt rules. Journalists often operate within large, centralized institutions that can gather, compile, distribute their work and collect money for it: networks, newspapers, press agencies. Critics on both left and right are deeply sceptical about those institutions. But there are still good reasons to believe, say, Andrew Marr reporting on politics for the BBC, or Mark Tully on India, or I. F. Stone or Seymour Hersh in Washington, not just because they know more than I do, or because they are there on the spot, but because they are experienced in gathering this kind of news; they know when a press release or speech has been timed as a distraction, when this person has said this sort of thing before, or when a statement of this kind from this kind of person is unusual. The weary cynicism that goes with the stereotype of reporters is their greatest asset; they do this for a living, and have seen it before, so at their best, they can spot a smear, or spin, or a distraction.

Let us apply this scepticism to a kind of writing that any of us might do. Part of learning to become an academic – even if only temporarily, to get a grade on a course – is to learn how to evaluate different kinds of texts that one might cite in building's one's own case: older and newer, popular vs. specialist writing, commercial vs. government vs. academic sources, more and less prestigious journals, more and less solid data and research methods. I wince, and sometimes comment, when a student cuts and pastes a bit from a web page with a vague source when I know there is a good academic article on the same topic. Authority in academic writing does have something to do with countable citations in academic journals, but it is not reducible to citations, job titles, institutional names or awards. It is a constantly reconstructed and revised standing of scholars among their peers. Academics say that they decide what to believe, in their specialties, on the basis of evidence, and that may be true for the immediate subfields in which we work. But for much of our academic lives, we rely on authorities, people whose past research and respect from their specialist communities mean that they are worth listening to.

Compare these kinds of authority to the 'Authority' calculated by *Technorati*, as a basis for presenting its search for blogs. For them, Authority is just the number of other blogs linking to this one, so *Instapundit* and *BoingBoing* have a lot, and most blogs have very little. Similarly, *Digg* and other news sites promote or relegate a story based, not on the judgement of human editors, but on the number of page views or the votes of readers. They would argue that with so many readers, the repeated visits indicate something about the interest of the material. What it doesn't indicate, as journalists point out, is how reliable or insightful that material is. *Instapundit* gets a lot of hits because Glenn Reynolds is witty, tireless, wide-ranging, because he projects an interesting personality, and because a lot of people agree with his views, not because any story he picks out is true, or is as important as he says it is (And to be fair, he never presents himself as an expert, except, occasionally, when he touches on his academic field of regulatory law).

Institutions such as the press, academia, medicine and law develop hierarchies of credibility, and the blogosphere flattens them out, so that anyone can say anything. There is little explicit evaluation of sources, based on their qualifications or experience or past record. There is little hedging of one's own statements to signal how far one would stand behind them. What counts is attention: the links of other bloggers, hits, track-backs, mentions in one of the top blogs. And statements stand out, not by what they add to what we know, but by their relation to our expectations. Audience design becomes the only constraint.

These changes are part of a broader change in our culture, one that includes rolling news, reality TV shows, focus groups in political campaigns: the flattening of credibility so that any contribution can mean as much as any other. In some sense that is liberating; no one denies that the institutions of the media, academia and the professions can be exclusive, elitist, self-interested and biased. But they can't all be replaced with a Google search. Bloggers don't worry much about getting the facts right, because they only ever present them as provisional, time-bound, limited. Or they see them as 'factoids', like the little bits on the front page of *USA Today*, statistics taken out of all context. It may be that such facts are harder to challenge, and that their rapid circulation makes them harder to recall. There are already many examples of rumours about political candidates, vaccinations, diets or events that prove impossible to kill once they are out there in the blogosphere. Chapter 9, on *Wikipedia*, looks again at issues around the collective production of facts.

8.10 What I did

For this chapter, I took the coding I had done for Chapter 7, and looked especially at the examples I had coded as *epistemic stance*. I categorized examples of evidentials as based on induction, deduction, hearsay and belief. Then I went back and checked all uses of certain markers, such as *of course*, *the fact that* and *in fact*. Evidentials, like other indicators of stance, are very unevenly distributed; as my examples suggest, there were a lot of them in *BoingBoing* and *Cosmic Variance* (with their technological and scientific discourse) and relatively few in *Bitch PhD*, *Black Prof* and *Raising Yousuf*, which involve more direct assertion.

8.11 What I read

Allan has the best overview of online journalism (2006); there are also useful comments on blogs and journalism in Gillmor (2004), Singer (2006), Bruns (2008), and an *Economist* special issue (Kluth 2006) that draws on a report on usage of online news (Project for Excellence in Journalism 2006). Zelizer (2004) provides review of the academic literature on journalism that raises many of the issues of factuality discussed here. For discussion of multiple public discourses with different norms for evidence, and the ways they become successful or don't see Warner (2002).

On stance, see the readings listed in Chapter 7. I have drawn on Chafe (1986) for my framework on signalling evidentiality. Much more detailed approaches to analysis of hedges, modals and other indications of stance will be found in other studies (e.g., Channell 1994; Stubbs 1996; Hyland 1998; Fairclough 2003). For implicatures and defeasiblity, see Levinson, *Pragmatics* (1983) and the original treatment (as *cancelability*) in Grice (1989: 44–46).

9 Collaboration: 'History' pages on *Wikipedia*

The chapter in a sentence: The History pages of Wikipedia *allow us to trace the processes through which the article we see was created, by additions, changes, formatting, proofreading – and some vandalism and reversion.*

A friend was reading a novel set in Italy, written in 1900, that referred to a disastrous war going on in Ethiopia. She knew about the terrible campaign in the 1930s, but not about this one, so she typed a phrase from the novel, 'Battle of Adwa' into Google, and got an article in *Wikipedia*, which linked to another article on 'The First Italo-Ethiopian War'. That did the job: the wider disputes, the campaign, the disposition of troops, the aftermath in Italian public opinion. Of course she could have gone to the university library and looked up histories of Ethiopia, biographies of the writer, studies of Italian politics, scholarly articles on the wider geopolitical context of the war as presaging the end of imperialism. But she got enough to go back to her novel. I suppose almost anyone who is not opposed in principle to *Wikipedia* (and some who are) has found an article that met a need at that moment; for me they might include 'Amor de Cosmos', 'H-Index', 'Comoros Islands' and 'Oxford Comma'. In each case I got a short introduction to the topic and a few facts (dates for the first, originator for the second, location for the third and style sheets for the last).

Yet I know there are criticisms of *Wikipedia*, and if I didn't, there is an article in *Wikipedia* that collects them ('Criticism of *Wikipedia*', which begins with a warning label, 'This article may be too long'). *Wikipedia* gets things wrong, indulges in triviality (or endless debates about the 'notability' or a band or high school or place), follows the biases of its users, and allows cults, flame wars and vandalism, and is too tolerant of some bizarre conspiracy theories. As an example of the many critics, I will quote a blog entry by David Crystal, because he is not only a respected linguist, he has edited encyclopaedias:

> My entry – as virtually every Wiki entry I have ever read – is a fascinating, unpredictable, dangerous selection of facts and fictions.

And the problem is, you never know which is which. It's not as if accurate information isn't available, especially these days, when official websites exist for most things. It takes a lot of time and effort and professionalism to compile encyclopedia entries which are balanced, objective, and accurate, and even then, the professionals don't always get it right. Wiki's fond hope is that by letting everyone have a go, eventually the truth will emerge, and the result will be better than the traditional encyclopedia. That was always a naive belief. (Crystal 2007)

I come back to these criticisms at the end of the chapter. For now I will just point out that *Wikipedia* is not a matter of 'letting everyone have a go'; instead a complex process of collaboration has emerged, based partly on some explicit principles and procedures, but more on a implicit sense of how they should interact. In this chapter, I would like to look in closer detail at what is revised and who does the revisions. As we will see, it takes a lot of people to keep the project going, adding facts (or what someone thinks is a fact), correcting where knowledge is contested, clarifying organization and style where different people have contributed different bits, and fending off vandals who want to wreck the entry and zealots who want to use it for their own purposes. In this chapter I will look at the histories of two Featured Articles.

In Chapter 10 I will look at how people keep this interaction going. Reading the 'User' pages that Wikipedians have posted to give information about themselves, one sees that many participants who have worked for many hours a week on *Wikipedia*, over several years, finally get fed up with what they consider to be the pettiness, obsessions, bias, ignorance and rudeness of other editors, and stop participating. Some sort of 'civility' (as *Wikipedia* calls it), and some sense of participation in a project with shared norms and goals, are necessary for *Wikipedia* to get better rather than worse over time. In Chapter 10 I will broaden out from the two articles in this chapter and consider the discussion pages of 20 articles, to see what Wikipedians argue about and how they argue.

9.1 How *Wikipedia* grows

I have chosen two articles and looked at the first 100 edits: one on the UK city 'Manchester' and one on the New York office building '7 World Trade Center'. The two articles developed differently. Editors of 'Manchester' worried mainly about how they should collect and organize the vast number of possible facts about a major urban centre and its history; it is largely a matter of collaboration (though there is one particular fact about which they kept, and keep, arguing). Editors of '7 World Trade Center' dealt from early on with differing points of view; their problem was how to include or exclude these points of view in an article representing a consensus. I am looking only at the first stage of development; much later, both were chosen as 'Featured Articles' after a review process, so they eventually met *Wikipedia*'s highest criteria for content, format and readability (only about 3,000, or about one in a thousand, articles have reached this level).

The data for such comparisons are easily available, but can be overwhelming. The 'History' page of a *Wikipedia* article saves every version that has existed of that article, shows what changes were made between any two versions, and shows what other edits that editor has made in their career (or, if they choose not to give themselves a name, what other edits have been done from that IP address). Editors usually give a brief characterization of their edit (they might say 'corrected typos in lead') and if they think more explanation is needed, they may post a comment on the 'Talk' page. 'Manchester' is one of the few articles on British cities to have achieved Featured Article status. The article began with a 'stub' (the most basic level of article) posted by *Alex* at 3:32 p.m. on 10 October 2001 (nine months after *Wikipedia* was founded).

Introduction

City in the Metropolitan Bourough of Greater Manchester, in the North West of England

History
Medieval
Roman
Manchester was occupied by Romans (know as 'Cair mauiguid'?).
A facsimile of a Roman fort exists in Castlefield (hence the name!)

Industrial Revolution
Manchester was a key part of the Industrial Revolution. Its damp climate made it and the surrounding area ideal for cotton mills. Its growth was also aided its proximity to Liverpools ports and the emerging rail and canal networks.

Trivia
Two football clubs Manchester United F.C. and Manchester City F.C.
4 Universities: University of Manchester (sometimes known locally as 'Owens', after its founder), UMIST, Manchester Metropolitan University and Salford University.

Links
Manchester City Council http://www.manchester.gov.uk
Manchester Online http://www.manchesteronline.co.uk

(http://en.*Wikipedia*.org/w/index.php?title=Manchester&oldid=267870)

This, as one of the early editors, Khendon, says, 'Needs expanding *lots* ...' In fact, it needed several stages of work, building up details, editing them into sections, rewriting lists as paragraphs and paragraphs as lists, hiving off daughter articles, and clarifying the style to make it more readable. The article was edited more than 5,200 times before it was chosen as a Featured Article 6 years later.

I came to the '7 World Trade Center' article through a list of Featured Articles in Art and Architecture, though it soon became apparent that most editors were interested in its history, not in its architecture (which, as far as I can tell, is undistinguished). Unlike the 'Manchester' page, which was created by a registered user who returned to check on it, '7 World Trade Center' was created at an anonymous IP address, on 6 September 2003:

> There are two building named 7 World Trade Center:
>
> The first building, built 1984–1986 and completed in March 1987 and collapsed on [[Semptember 11], [[2001].
>
> The second building, a rebuild replacement for the origianl, to be complete be 2005.

Not surprisingly, he or she then goes on to make six revisions correcting spelling and grammatical errors (see if you can spot them). Five months later, *Rbs* says 'a few details, but still a stub' (the most basic grade of article). There were about 1,800 edits before it was approved as a featured article in September 2007; when it was on the main page in November, it got more than 20 edits in one day.

I will summarize the first 100 edits in each article as *adding* information (34 edits in 'Manchester', 27 in '7 World Trade Center', *changing* the information (24 and 16), *formatting* to fit *Wikipedia* conventions (7 and 11), *proofreading* (12 and 17), *vandalism* (2 and 3) and *reversion* (2 and 12). These changes followed somewhat different patterns in the two articles.

i. Adding

'Manchester' starts slowly, and editors generally add information to fill out existing lists. After 10 October 2001, *Alex*'s first page sits there untouched (except for his own correction) for seven months. Then *64.26.98.90* starts of a list of towns named 'Manchester' in the US; the same IP address comes back through the next months adding smaller and smaller places (17 July 2002). *Khendon* adds a number of details about the city, including a mention of the 1996 IRA bombing and the crucial statement at the beginning, 'It is the second largest conurbation in the United Kingdom' (20 September 2002). (This sentence sets off a dispute that, as we will see, continues to run while I am writing this.) A few days later, *62.60.43.89* adds that 'Manchester is the location for the fictional borough of Wetherfield, home of Coronation Street', a long-running TV soap opera (26 September 2002), starting off a series of popular culture links, and the month after that *Sjc* adds a sentence saying 'It has played a significant role in British youth and counterculture in recent years', followed by examples of three rock bands and three 'punk rock outfits' (26 September 2002). So in its first year, the article has been edited only occasionally, but its lists invite additions and modifications.

Later additions follow this pattern of modifying what is there: more about the bombing (*Alex* again, 20 October 2002), details about canals that start lists on transport (*Renata*, 1 November 2002), links for the Hallé Orchestra and its home in the Bridgewater Hall (*Camembert,* 16 March 2003), for the Romans and the airport (*G-Man* , 21 June 2003), and later for Free Trade Hall (*R. Lowry*, 24 January 2004). *152.163.252.38* adds that it is 'Next to the city of Salford', starting off a flurry of additions of other towns nearby (1 July 2003). *80.255* adds that Manchester is 'in the traditional county of Lancashire', which is a more contentious issue than it seems (26 October 2003). (Note for the confused: Manchester was for hundreds of years part of Lancashire, before local government reorganization in 1974 put it in its own county. Some people, as we will see, feel strongly about this.) *Morwen* adds a map, the first illustration, showing Manchester city within the Greater Manchester area (25 January 2004). Each of these editors starts lists that carry over in some form or another to sections in the later featured article. IBM researchers have noted in a quantitative study a 'first mover advantage' in which those who post first have more of their words retained through many page views (Viégas, Wattenberg and Dave 2004). Here we see that they have, in addition, a tendency to set the agenda for later contributors, whether it is the centrality of the IRA bomb or the need to list rock bands.

The agenda for '7 World Trade Center' is set in different ways: most additions deal directly or indirectly with one issue: the collapse of the building on September 11, 2001. In fact, *Qaless* adds a reference to September 11 six minutes after the page was created. Some details seem straightforward enough for a skyscraper. *Rbs* adds some details about size of the buildings (10 February), *12.144.5.2* adds the height in feet (28 June), *Dalton* adds a link to photos (12 September 2004),

133

68.193.167.214 mentions that the film *Working Girl* was shot at the old building (27 December 2004), *Hyperbole* adds a list of tenants (22 July 2005). But alongside these occasional additions are comments on the owner (18 April 2004), an extensive summary of a scene from PBS documentary on the conspiracy theory (28 May 2004), mention that the CIA was a tenant (13 July 2004), a magazine with an article that mentions the conspiracy (19 March 2005), and finally a very long rant summarizing the conspiracy (9 July 2005). To understand all these added details, one has to see that almost any addition can support the view that the building collapsed after being hit by debris from the World Trade Center and the resulting fire, or the view that it was deliberately destroyed by controlled demolition. (See the differing uses of added details in Table 9.1.)

And each of these additions leads on into subsidiary arguments and supporting details. One could go on and on – and they do. Every fact is charged with its meaning in a potential conspiracy, and every revision is scrutinized for the intentions of the editor. The stakes are high: from the point of view of those who see the collapse as controlled demolition, most editors on *Wikipedia*, along with most other media (apart from a few articles) are supporting a plot against democracy leading to the highest levels of government. From the point of view of those who see the collapse as resulting from the impact of debris and the subsequent fire, *Wikipedia* is in danger of being used as a soapbox for the rants of a tiny minority who have no interest in the project of an encyclopaedia.

Table 9.1 *Two views of the events at 7 World Trade Center*

Fire	Demolition
Gash was caused by debris	Gash is not visible in this picture (provides picture)
Video shows the building fell slowly	Video shows the building fell quickly
FEMA found no evidence of demolition	FEMA director said he was puzzled by the evidence
The building owner said 'Pull it' (quoted in a later documentary) to get the firefighters out of the building	'Pull it' was a command to pull the building down, so the building owner is admitting that there was a plan devised earlier
List of tenants includes many corporations and agencies	List of agencies includes the CIA
Diesel fuel may have fed the fire, so heat would be enough to cause a collapse	Fires burned only 20 minutes at each location, so they could not have caused the collapse, so it must have been something else
Building was cantilevered over an electricity substation, making it easier for the damage to cause a collapse	Building fell into its own footprint instead of falling over, which is what happens in a controlled explosion

ii. Changing

There is one point on which 'Manchester' is also controversial: the population in relation to that of other British cities. The problem here is the same as it would be for Boston or San Francisco; the political district of the city is only a small part of a much larger urban area. We have seen that *Khendon* said on 20 September 2002 that Manchester was 'the centre of the second largest conurbation in the United Kingdom'. Five days later, *172.181.80.253* changes it to say 'third largest conurbation. Only London and Birmingham are larger'. The next morning, *Khendon* changes it back, and within four hours, *Chris Q* changes it again, saying 'Decided to be bold – I am sure it is the third largest'. Less than half an hour later, *Khendon* comes up with a compromise statement that lasts for a while: 'London is larger, and the Birmingham area is sometimes considered larger, depending on the exact method of counting'. Half an hour later he adds the population figure, 40,000, unfortunately dropping a digit. This stays for three weeks (the longest an outright error remained in this period), until *Sjc* corrects it on 19 October. Further slight modifications come on 1 July 2003, 9 November, 24 December (gosh, he's editing this on Christmas Eve!) and regularly through the entire history of the article. *G-Man* tries to justify using the larger figures for the whole metropolitan area by saying 'The word "Manchester" is often used to refer to the entire Greater Manchester conurbation'. And then this sentence itself becomes a locus for changes (for instance, the substitution of 'normally' for 'often'). There is a similar sort of controversy about status on the 'Talk' pages of the article for nearly every large US city: whether the article name should give the state (Seattle, Washington) or the city alone (Seattle). For every city name that is not ambiguous (like 'Portland' or 'Boston'), someone insists that being known as just 'Seattle' is essential to its being a major world city. Editors move the main article from one title to the other, leaving a redirect, until someone stops them.

Other changes are less controversial matters of correction. *Renata* corrects the Roman name (29 October 2002), and later (4 December) she points out that Coronation Street is set in Salford (the neighbouring borough of Greater Manchester). Similarly, *217.155.205.64* says that the Manchester United football ground, Old Trafford, is actually in the neighbouring borough of Trafford. And some issues are controversial for a few editors. *G-Man*, in the course of some stylistic revision, and perhaps unintentionally, deletes the reference at the beginning to the historic county of Lancashire (26 November 2003). But as we will see in the next chapter, some people believe that the historical counties (superceded in 1974) are still the real divisions around with the geography of

England is oriented. There are also a few deletions for stylistic reasons; the very first version said there was a Roman fort in Castlefield ('Hence the name!'). *Renata* deletes this parenthetical aside as inappropriate to an encyclopaedia.

As one might expect from what we saw of the additions, the changes in '7 World Trade Center' are more contentious, and almost none of them have to do with readability. On 28 May 2004, *66.143.155.193* adds a reference to an interview with Larry Silverstein, the building's owner:

> In the interview, he admits that WTC7 was 'pulled', that is, intentionally demolished.

In the video link, Mr Silverstein does say that he then said 'pull it'. The 'admits' and the explanation that this was a command to demolish the building are the editor's addition. Within six minutes, *Rickyrab* has rewritten the sentence:

> In the video he says there was a 'pulling' at WTC 7, which some people interpret as meaning that it was intentionally demolished.

Here the (remembered and reported) command is turned into a gerund ('pulling'), and what for the first editor was a reformulation of the words is treated as just one interpretation ('Some people' is a common way of putting a minority view, so common that *Wikipedia* discourages its use on its list of 'WP: Weasel Words'). Later *216.145.49.15* deletes the paragraphs on 'pull it' (12 November 2004), and then two weeks later *Rebroad* puts it back in (1 December). Then *68.101.163.141* adds the sentence:

> Alternatively, the expression could simply refer to the decision to pull firefighters out of the building. (16 December 2004)

Two months later, *216.174.53.110* rewrites the whole section on collapse, supporting the controlled demolition argument (for instance, the debris from one of the twin towers now falls 'near' rather than 'on' WTC 7. (You begin to get the argument now? If it didn't fall on the building, it couldn't have been responsible for the fires and collapse, so one must look for other sinister forces behind it.) Then *ProhibitOnions*, saying he 'Tided up section', makes changes that support the view that it collapsed (29 April 2005). This goes on and on with large changes and small. Conspiracy theorists keep adding links to 9/11 conspiracy sites, and others take them out. '*Many* have questioned why it finally fell' is changed to '*Conspiracy theorists* have questioned why it finally fell', and then to '*many (including conspiracy theorists)*, have questioned . . . [my italics]'. The sentence in the article as it stands on the day I am writing this (19 November 2008) is '*Conspiracy theorists* believe the building collapses on September 11, including that of *building seven*, were the result of *controlled demolition*', with links to other articles at each of the underlined phrases, and four references to sources outside *Wikipedia*. One has to look at the 'History' pages to see that the apparent stability of the page I see today is the result of a torrent of changes, and a dialogue in which each change responds to other changes and is addressed to other editors.

iii. Formatting

Some changes do not change the information in an article, but change the structure, or make the article conform to *Wikipedia* conventions. As other researchers have noted, there are relatively few moves of whole sections within articles (Viégas, Wattenberg and Dave 2004). Viégas and her colleagues suggest that this may be because the editing screen on *Wikipedia* only has 20 lines, so that even articles as short as 'Manchester' and '7 World Trade Center' are at this stage are not entirely visible within the window. There are only two significant moves in the first hundred changes in 'Manchester': *Morwen* adds a heading for 'Transport', (24 January 2004) and *R Lowry* moves that section after 'History' (1 February 2004). Other changes include moving whole sections on subordinate topics to new, related 'daughter' articles (e.g., 'Manchester Airport') and disambiguation of links ('Oasis', 'Football'). The list of US cities named Manchester (one of the most frequent sites of additions) is moved to a separate disambiguation page, and the list of nearby towns (another very active section) is replaced by a standard template of 'Districts of Northwest England' at the bottom of the page. There would be much more of this sort of change in 2007, to prepare the article for 'Good Article' and 'Featured Article' status, and try to conform to all the *Wikipedia* format conventions.

As one can imagine from the previous sections on additions and changes, even format questions in '7 World Trade Center' are controversial. An early redirect, deleting the whole article and referring it to 'World Trade Center' implies that, though this building was built and rebuilt separately from the twin towers, it is notable only as part of their story (and conspiracy). It is reverted within two minutes. Later editors suggest that added material on controlled demolition should be moved to 9/11 conspiracy articles. The heading of the middle section as introduced by *Sfoskett* (10 September 2004) is 'Destruction of 7 World Trade Center', which allows either reading. Later *216.174.53.17* reinstates deleted conspiracy material under the heading 'Contorversy' (*sic*). The current heading for the section is 'Collapse', which effectively sidelines the controlled demolition reading, which as we have seen, is developed only in links. The opening paragraphs before the table of contents, called the *lead*, are seen as most crucial in long articles; in controversial articles, the changes often consist of moving a statement into or out of the lead.

iv. Proofreading

In 'Manchester', the very first change made is *Alex* correcting some of his own typos. Most spelling mistakes are corrected fairly quickly, by the person who made them or someone else, but a correction of 'recieved' to 'received' took four months. Editors change punctuation; *G-Man* inserts a comma after 'Manchester' in his own sentence 'The word Manchester, is often used . . .' (which, by the way, is not correct punctuation). In '7 World Trade Center', as we have seen, the first version was also typo-laden. Again, most writers correct their typos as soon as they have saved them to the article (a 'hoist of unrelated businesses' rather than a 'host'). Other editors correct italicization of titles or format of links.

v. Vandalism

A comparison of the two pages shows that it can be difficult to determine just what is vandalism, intended only to damage the article. The first incontestable vandalism on 'Manchester' comes at the end of my sample, after the article had been up for two and a half years. At 13:37 on 8 March 2004, 'JOE IS FUCKING WANK' is inserted by *212.219.39.100*; it is reverted by *P. T. Aufrette* at 13:38. The vandal is back in the next minute with 'JOE SLATER IS A WANKER HA HAHAHAHAHAHH GAY', and is reverted at 13:39 by *Tannin*. There is a third attempt, and the vandal goes away. The example conforms to the figures presented by the IBM team, showing that major vandalism is typically reverted within two minutes, and within a minute if it contains an obscenity (Viégas, Wattenberg and Dave 2004).

It can be harder to tell what is vandalism on the '7 World Trade Center' article, and what is just strongly held opinion. On 27 April 2005, *211.26.48.3* adds the sentence at the end of the section 'The Destruction of 7 World Trade Center' saying 'This is of course a lie. The building was demolished'. They violate basic *Wikipedia* conventions: adding an assertion that is a point of view, without a source, rudely assuming motivation ('lie') and assuming that others must agree ('of course'), and not checking the 'Talk' pages for earlier discussion of this issue. But they do not intend simply to disrupt the page, as did the vandal on

138

'Manchester'; they intend to promote what they think is the truth, or rather THE TRUTH. We can see editors trying to determine whether new contributors are trying to help or disrupt. On 9 July 2005 an anonymous IP adds 661 words of conspiracy theory, not integrated into the article, saying that the Federal Emergency Management Agency 'admitted' its role in the conspiracy, and ending 'God Bless America and the Truth can set you free'. *JimWae*, who has been trying to revise passages to be what he considers even-handed in their treatment, at first tries to reason with them as he reverts the page: 'Comments belong on Talk page – "admitted" is either POV or wrong word to use' (see Chapter 10 for the use of 'POV'). Nine minutes later the same IP puts it back; it is reverted again by *Jimbobsween* (in 6 minutes) and is put back on again in 11 minutes by someone with the name (apparently invented for this particular edit) *Capitalcrime*. At this point, *JimWae*, reverting it for a third time, comments '(guess it's just vandalism – not unfamiliarity with talk pages & encyclopedia)'. *JimWae* decides it is vandalism, not on the basis of its content, but because the editor seems unwilling to engage with other editors in making the article. Charges of 'vandalism' are typically hurled back and forth by both sides in a controversy; *Capitalcrime* could say that it is vandalism to revert their work.

After 100 edits, both pages have the basics of an entry – location, some history, some relevant topics that would be developed. The editing would intensify in later stages (when there might be 100 edits in 2 days, or in 2 hours, not 2 years). By the time they achieve Featured Article status, they are hardly recognizable. 'Manchester' has many more sections, all in paragraph rather than list form, and many daughter articles (e.g., 'Culture of Manchester', 'History of Manchester'). '7 World Trade Center' has a great deal of architectural and engineering information on both buildings, and the conspiracy theory has been reduced to a short paragraph. But both articles still contain much of the wording proposed in the early edits, and the 'Talk' pages are still full of arguments about population (for 'Manchester') and 'pull it' (for '7 World Trade Center').

9.2 Who edits?

The History page lists users who did these edits, and the names link, in most cases, to editors' self-descriptions on their User pages. We find a mix of contributors: *frequent editors* who take some responsibility for the page, *occasional editors* who drop in to change a detail here or there, *adminstrators* who check for format and mediate controversies, and the occasional *vandal*. They are distributed rather differently on the two pages; 'Manchester' has an emerging core of editors, some of whom are still working on it 4 years later, while almost all edits of '7 World Trade Center' are made by one-off contributors. You have probably noticed that I have referred to most of the '7WTC' editors by their IP addresses. Lots of regular *Wikipedia* editors prefer not to register and take a name, but in this case, the IP addresses were typically used only on a few days, or for one evening, or just for this edit. That means the editors have no long-term commitment to the development of the article; they just want to get their point across in as many places as possible.

Several kinds of Wikipedians regularly contribute to the first 100 edits of 'Manchester'. *Alex*, who starts the page, is from Manchester and is by his own description a computer geek. (He also has this message for people like me who look up his user page: 'If you want to know more about random people you have come across on the 'net you should probably get out more'.) *Khendon*, *Chris Q* and *G-Man* are examples of editors who check back on the article once in a while; Chris Q is from Yorkshire and G-Man from Rugby, so they are committed to *Wikipedia*, not just to their local community. *Lexor*'s other edits are usually in articles about music. *Renata* lives in Edinburgh, but has an interest in canals that explains her first edit; she then stays on to make some other changes. *Morwen* lists on her page lots of books on local government; she is the one who comes up with the map of the district.

The interests of some of the editors of '7 World Trade Center' can also be seen on their user pages. All we know about the creator of the page, IP *171.75.72.114*, is that he or she only used this address that evening, and other edits include articles for 'Osama bin Laden', 'Al Qaeda' 'World Trade Center' and (one of the most revised articles in all of *Wikipedia*) 'September 11, 2001 attacks'. The user at IP *68.193.167.214* mainly edits articles about New York City buildings and subways. *68.193.167.214* usually edits articles on films involving New York. *Pedant* has an article on 9/11 conspiracies on his user page. *JimWae* usually works on articles concerned with religion or with Taiwan; I don't find any indication of a special interest in this topic.

There is another group of editors who are interested in the format and style rather than the content of the article. On 'Manchester', *AntonioMartin* has never been to the UK (according to his user page), but can add a cross-reference. *Mav* and *Warofdreams* are administrators, very experienced editors who have been given the right to arbitrate in conflicts and block vandals. The editors who deal so quickly with the vandal are in Canada and Australia, respectively. On '7 World Trade Center', *Simon P* is an administrator (with 94,000 edits!) who labels the article a stub, while a year later *Modster* removes the tag. *Fvw* and *Andrew Pmk* say on their user pages that they mostly revert vandalism (other editors give them awards for this service). *Jason One* goes around italicizing movie titles.

Finally there are the vandals. The user page for the IP address of the 'Manchester' vandal also shows a list of edits, so we can follow the train of his or her (surely his?) changes through a whole range of articles (why oh why pick on 'Art Deco'?) His contributions are always this sort of schoolboy graffiti, and they are generally corrected this quickly, so he goes away. Finally the IP address is blocked from editing *Wikipedia*, though of course he could just find another computer. The rants added to '7 World Trade Center' are harder to trace; the IP address shows no history, the same user apparently moves from one machine to another nearby, and the new names they apparently make up link to nothing. On *Wikipedia* and on the web more generally, this switching between IP addresses and names is called *sock puppetry* – that is, creating a new web identity (a cheap puppet) just to talk through it without revealing one's own identity.

9.3 Revision and facts

I chose 'Manchester' and '7 World Trade Center' to be broadly representative of the first stage of *Wikipedia* articles. Some of the points I have made about these articles apply to most or all of the other 18 *Wikipedia* articles I studied (see Chapter 10):

- The articles start with a very basic stub, not an extended article by one person (Some, for instance 'Mary Wollstonecraft' start with a big chunk of non-copyright text that is then revised).
- There are relatively few edits in the early period of the entry, and edits cluster at a few periods of activity.
- Early edits set up wording and categories that often survive in later versions, even after the thousands of edits needed to make a featured article.
- Correction of vandalism and the more obvious spelling mistakes happens very quickly (though 'recieve' persisted for months).
- For 'Manchester' and most articles (but not '7 World Trade Center' in the stage I considered), a committed group of heavy editors makes most of the edits.
- Almost any article seems to find, at some point, a controversial angle (for instance, the, 'Washington' in the 'Seattle' article).

I think I am now justified in adding one more bullet point to this list: 'the process works'. The articles I looked at have, at some point or another in their development, plenty of factual errors, biases, typos and rants. Some would argue that they include topics that are too trivial to be worth writing about at all. But as these articles evolve, the entries get longer, better, more balanced, more cautious, and sometimes, more coherent. Mistakes are corrected. Sources are questioned. Categories are reconsidered. Vandals and nuts are seen off (though they return again).

My assertion that 'the process works', even in qualified form, applies only to articles that are edited a lot, but not too much. Hundreds of thousands of articles on *Wikipedia* are stubs that sit there unedited from month to month; if no one checks them, there is no reason to have any faith at all in their content. And hundreds of articles are so controversial and vandal-prone that they must always be used with caution; I am not sure what one could learn from 'George W. Bush' or 'Jesus' after the smoke of battle has cleared. And I would hope that any reader of this chapter would realize that the article one sees in *Wikipedia* is not as stable as it may look. So far we have looked at only part of the process. We have seen that some edits survive, while others are rejected immediately, and that out of this process a text emerges over time. But we haven't seen why some edits are accepted, what arguments Wikipedians use when they disagree, or how they maintain a sense of a shared project in all this discord. To see these processes, we will turn from the 'History' to the 'Talk' pages in the Chapter 10.

9.4 What I did

I chose 'Manchester' for close attention to the 'History' pages because it wasn't (I thought) a particularly controversial topic; '7 World Trade Center' is an example of a featured article that is controversial. (I couldn't use US cities for this purpose, because as I have mentioned in the chapter, they are usual subject to continual redirects, between for instance 'Seattle' and 'Seattle, Washington', that make their history hard to follow.) I looked at the first 100 edits of articles on the 'History' pages. I followed up 'User' pages from the 'History' pages, where each has a link, to find out what else that editor had edited.

9.5 What I read

Wikis seem to have attracted better academic studies, so far, than blogs. That may be because *Wikipedia* provides such great data for a study. I used to spend hours and days and weeks comparing two versions of a poem or an essay or a scientific article. So I am astonished to find (as I said in 'What I did') that *Wikipedia* has a history page with all previous versions lined up (that alone can take a literary scholar or a discourse analyst weeks to prepare), and then it will compare any two versions and point out the changes. And it says who made the changes, and links to their page, where one can often find what other edits they have made. This huge body of data has been used by a group at IBM Research Laboratories to make 'History Flow' visualizations that show how an article develops (Viégas, Wattenberg and Dave 2004; Viégas, Wattenberg, Kriss and van Ham 2007). Those are the most heavily cited studies, and they are lovely to look at too. The data have also been used (along with some statistics on page views that one can't find on a *Wikipedia* history page) by Priedhorsky and his colleagues to show the build-up of information on articles, and the effects of vandalism (Priedhorsky et al. 2007). Pfeil, Zaphiris and Ang correlated the kinds of changes made in the different language editions with traits of national cultures drawn from Hofstede (Pfeil et al. 2006). And John Jones has used the information in the editors' comments to categorize the kinds of revisions made (for instance, macro or micro) in Featured Articles and articles that didn't get FA status (Jones 2008); he finds the ones that failed usually didn't get edited enough beyond the stage of being lists of information. Emigh and Herring (2005) compare the statistics on article length, word length and various qualitative stylistic features, for *Wikipedia*, *Everything2* (which I hadn't heard of) and the *Columbia Encyclopedia*, reminding me that *Wikipedia*'s collaborative process is not the only way to do it.

There have also been studies of authorship that go beyond this huge trove of data. Bryant, Forte and Bruckman (2005) interviewed Wikipedians, and they show some interesting differences of perspective between novice and experienced users. Rosenzweig (2006) has a thoughtful piece that goes beyond his immediate concern, knowledge about history (He was the first, I think, to raise issues about the style of *Wikipedia* entries). There have been many magazine articles on *Wikipedia*, but he most informative and enthusiastic is the novelist Nicholson Baker's review in the *New York Review of Books*, which captures some of the obsessional quality of editing (2008). He's reviewing Broughton (2008), which is more than it seems from the title, not just a user's manual, but a thoughtful guide to the phenomenon and the practices of Wikipedians. And of the many books coming out now on *Wikipedia*, the most interesting comments are from Axel Bruns (2008).

And then there are the critics. Most just give a sort of gut response, without much argument or experience with wikis, but I have found

interesting remarks in articles by two experienced editors of print encyclopaedias (McHenry 2004; Crystal 2007), and in the criticisms by Jaron
Lanier (2006) and the responses to them by defenders of *Wikipedia* and
other Web 2.0 developments.

10 Arguing: 'Talk' pages on *Wikipedia*

__The chapter in a sentence:__ When Wikipedians argue, they refer to the explicit 'Principles' of Wikipedia *as shared knowledge, and they also draw on an implicit rhetoric of politeness that they refer to as 'Civility'.*

In Chapter 9, I looked at the 'History' pages of two *Wikipedia* articles. In this chapter, I look at the 'Talk' pages, where editors may (but do not have to) post comments on the changes they have made. These pages, with their dense exchanges about POV, NOR, RS, and UNDUE, their arguments about links and leads, might seem to be of interest only to *Wikipedia* insiders. But I recommend that students always check them, because they can quickly tell any casual browser something of the story behind this particular article, who has contributed, what people argue about, what they agree on, what sources they respect, why they think the topic matters – all information that might be missing in the rather dry article that has resulted. More than this, I will argue that the Talk pages tell us something about the *Wikipedia* in general, and how it works, because they show how people argue, how they interpret the principles underlying *Wikipedia*, how they treat each other, and what they think the project is about.

In Chapter 9, we saw that there were some serious disagreements in the first 100 edits on two articles. But even when there is something more at stake than whether Manchester is the Second City (or Third or Ninth) of the United Kingdom, it is hard to see why editors become so very angry. Take this exchange:

> –There seems to be a consensus here that it is a theory and I am going to be bold and add that into the text. The Person Who Is Strange
> –Things are not always as they seem (to you). – BozMo
> –To you as well. Could you explain to me why your opinion is more valid than mine? Because you follow what everyone else says? And also, who's that idiot who deleted my contributions to the page without even mentioning it in the talk page? So now global warming followers have more **rights** than I do? The Person Who Is Strange (*Global Warming*)

You might think that Global Warming is an important enough issue to get angry about. But consider this rebuke, with its mixture of excessive politeness and explicit rudeness, in which one of the targets (*80.255*) is the editor who added the fact that Manchester is in the traditional county of Lancashire:

> There would be no confusion at all if atavistic traditionalists like you and 80.255 didn't go around claiming that historical counties are real and current existing and holy and unalterable things. So please stop. <u>Morwen</u> (*Counties*)

But the anger in the exchanges I have just quoted is not just due to the issue; it is also clearly a matter of face, each person's desire to be seen in a favourable light, and to be allowed to act as they wish. *The Person Who Is Strange* (TPWIS) is personally insulted; Morwen puts her point in the most personal possible way ('atavistic traditionalists like you'). Why? They would not seem to have status to lose, a real name or institutional credentials to defend, or an investment of money to risk. But like all Wikipedians, they do have a something to lose: they have given it some time, they are known (if only by a nickname or IP address), and they are angry that all this work and reputation can be lost in a click from someone else. And there is a sense that all this is happening in public, even though any embarrassment may be in front of only a handful of *Wikipedians* (See 'What I read' for more on reputation and motivations).

But *TPWIS* is not just thinking of their own standing and freedom of action. They are angry that what they saw as a shared project is not shared by everyone. They think that it is a principle of *Wikipedia*, as it is of the blogosphere, that everyone has the right to be heard. It is not; on *Wikipedia*, anyone can contribute, but contributions are edited by others, and only with the agreement of others can one's own contribution stand. So there are two conceptions here of what makes something knowledge, and that, apparently, is worth some name-calling (as we will see). Wikipedians like *BazMo*, *The Person Who is Strange* and *Morwen* always need to argue passionately about changes, defending or attacking, while also presenting themselves as rational people committed to the shared project and observant of its rules.

10.1 How Wikipedians argue

Wikipedians use a full range of rhetorical devices: arguments by analogy, authority, cause and effect, classification, and attacks on the opponent or *ad hominems* (for instance when Morwen categorizes her opponent among 'atavistic traditionalists'). But they also have a specific rhetoric based on explicit 'principles', such as Neutral Point of View, No Original Research and Verifiability. From the first days of letting anyone do whatever they want, these principles have developed the way other *Wikipedia* pages have, by collaborative editing with a 'Talk' page and a 'History' page. Principles tend to be referred to by abbreviations, especially in the comment line of an edit: NPOV for Neutral Point of View. As you can imagine, the application of a principle in any particular case is debatable, and two opposite sides of an argument can present themselves as adhering to it. But they are usually not rejected outright, because they are seen as following from *Wikipedia*'s definition as an encyclopaedia. And they provide a useful basis for arguments, because one can expect other participants to recognize them: and if they don't, it suggests they are 'newbies', first-time editors who are unfamiliar with the conventions.

i. Neutral Point of View (W: NPOV)

The most frequently invoked, and most controversial, principle is that Wikipedia should have a 'Neutral Point of View' (NPOV). It is of course obvious to any academic that this is impossible; knowledge is produced from a particular framework of assumptions and stance. It's obvious to Wikipedians too; they are well aware of the problems with any idea of neutrality or objectivity, but invoke it as an ideal specifically for writing encyclopaedia entries. It does not exclude all statements that could be challenged by someone, but means that editors of the text should try to include the full range of views on a topic, and exclude merely personal opinions. NPOV criticisms can be used in different ways. The acronym can even be used as a verb, so Rickyrab, replacing the conspiracy theory account of the video (see Chapter 9), says 'Trying to NPOV this' ('7 World Trade Center'). Someone who finds the 'Fluoxetine' article too negative says:

> I **NPOV** tagged it because there is nothing positive about it. From reading this article, one would think prozac is poison and eli lilly is an evil corporation bent on destroying lives in the name of profits. Lets have a fair article.67.167.130.247 ('Fluoxetine')

Often the charge that it is not a neutral point of view really means the writer finds the edit just wrong. Here the writer follows the tag with a direct threat to the original writer's face.

> The section on Estuary English is very **POV**. Whoever wrote it is trying to stating that such speakers don't understand grammar whereas it's quite clear that the writer doesn't understand it either. ('Accents')

POV can be invoked by both sides in a controversial exchange, because both sides see any concession to the other as moving the article away from a neutral middle. In the following example one editor, addressing another editor (MC), defends the addition of anti-vaccination material to the 'Vaccination' article by saying that otherwise it would be POV. He or she glosses the principle as saying they must describe the dispute.

> The lead was **POV** without those additions, MC, and basically read as though written by a pro-vaccination campaigner. We have to describe the dispute, not engage in it. ('Vaccination')

This example may seem to reveal a problem with NPOV; it guarantees a place for every dissenting view, conspiracy theory, or hobbyhorse. Balancing it is another principle, 'Undue Weight' (WP: UNDUE), that says that the views of a tiny minority should not be given equal space with those of a majority. Here the issue is the lead, the opening paragraph; MC would be happy to have this person's views opposing vaccination in the article, but not as the first thing. NPOV is a rhetorical device for relocating 'neutrality' close to one's own position, but it is also a necessary principle of an encyclopaedia. An editor tired of removing value-laden judgements from the article on 'Vegetarianism' says:

> In Huxley's Island, there are trained birds who flit about reminding people, 'Here and now, folks, here and now.' Sometimes I wish Wikipedia had a few digital birds to say 'NPOV, folks, NPOV.':) – FOo

ii. No Original Research (W: NOR)

Academics often criticize *Wikipedia* on the grounds that it is not peer reviewed. The criticism misses the point; as Axel Bruns points out, *Wikipedia* does not aim to produce knowledge, but to collect 'currently prevalent representations of knowledge about the world' (2008: 114). The principle applies even to facts that you might know personally, but can't document (for instance, a former pub licensee challenging a comment about the closing hours of campus bars at Lancaster University, or a professional radiographer citing CT scan dosages). One often sees criticisms that people are challenged even when editing an article on themselves, a topic on which they are assumed to be experts. But a few examples would show that one wouldn't want to accept living people as having the final word on the facts of their own lives. More commonly, the principle is invoked to exclude people with their own theories or speculations. For instance, on the 'Traveling Salesman Problem' 'Talk' page, a non-expert suggests a simple solution to this complex, central problem that has lots of mathematicians working on it. Another editor tactfully tells them that it *is* a solution, but not to this problem. In any case, the comment says, if they think they have a solution, they should publish it in a mathematics journal, not in *Wikipedia*. In 'Linguistics', Grick deletes a very long addition, without references, that opens 'At the beginning of the 21st century Su Cheng Zhong gave a new answer of what is "Linguistics"'. Grick comments:

> Wikipedia **is not a place for new ideas**, like these by 'Su Cheng Zhong.'

Mark Dingemanse adds, a few hours later, a reference to the relevant principles:

> See also *No original research* and Wikipedia:What Wikipedia is not. ('Linguistics')

Reference to the principles apparently makes further explanation of or apology for the deletion unnecessary. But as with NPOV, it is not always clear what constitutes NOR. The following example continues the dispute above, about vaccinations. A critic of vaccines wants to include a graph of declining death rates, and say that it shows that rates would have declined without vaccines; another editor responds that the graph is sourced but not this interpretation, so it is Original Research.

> –I agree: digging up arbitrary graphs from among the thousands published and making an argument for the non-effectiveness of vaccines is at least bordering on **original research**, and possibly more than just bordering on it . . . Delirium ('Vaccines')
> – . . . One more thing: a graph is not '**original research**' if all it does is present data. The interpretation is the research, and here we are presenting both sides' interpretation . . . Leifern ('Vaccines')

Leifern responds not to the NOR argument, but to NPOV: it is research, but the article can give both sides. So even with agreed principles, there is always disagreement about how they are applied.

iii. Verifiability

Complementing the convention of No Original Research is a convention saying that every statement must be verifiable. University students often ask if they have to have a citation for every sentence of their coursework essays, and lecturers may tell them that no, some statements are generally accepted within the discipline and need no citation. *Wikipedia* has no such out; one can always call for sources in a dispute. But such calls usually lead to another dispute, about sources.

Here *MastCell* challenges a citation to the *Journal of American Physicians and Surgeons*:

> I'm sorry, but the political agenda of JPandS is relevant (as one of their major political issues is anti-vaccinationism). The journal has a clearly stated political agenda, and the piece in question was, in fact, authored by someone with a legal rather than scientific or medical background. (*MastCell* 'Vaccination')

Putting 'citation needed' tags throughout an article can be a way of criticizing one position. In the 'Shakespeare' talk pages, *MarkThomas* says 'citation mania is usually a sign of POV'ist activity' and says that it would be wrong to give a separate citation of every fact in the early life:

> I am not arguing against **verifiability**, just making a suggestion about how the verifiability of the whole early life of Shakespeare, all of which is basically unverifiable by any provable source, be presented to our readers. ('Shakespeare')

MarkThomas is not saying that all the apparent facts of Shakespeare's life should be excluded (that is what those who propose rival candidates for authorship would say). He is arguing that the principle of Verifiability must be relative to the topic at hand.

Arguments about what counts as a legitimate source can lead us to real questions about how we get our information and what we trust (see Chapter 6). For instance, there were arguments about whether British tabloids could be used in the article on 'The Disappearance of Madeleine McCann', about an event in 2007 that was much reported in the press (later a UK court ruled that some of the reporting was libellous). And there were questions raised about the Guardian's story in February about Prozac; on the Talk pages it was argued that a reading of the published study did not support their interpretation. In practice, Verifiability leads to edit wars, but ideally, the effect of the principle is to push Wikipedians to critical views of available sources.

iv. Be bold

These three principles should be fairly uncontroversial, but there is one that really affronts some academics and defenders against barbarians at the gate: Be Bold. Wikipedia is based on the idea that it is better to say something roughly accurate, and have somebody else improve it, than to say nothing at all. When someone complains in the press of an inaccuracy (as David Crystal does in the blog quotation in Chapter 7), the response of Wikipedians is always that the complainant should just change it – it takes no special knowledge or skill to do it.

150

> If you feel a change is needed, feel free to make it yourself! Wikipedia is a <u>wiki</u> so anyone (yourself included) can edit any article by following the **Edit this page** link. . . . Wikipedia convention is to <u>be</u> <u>bold</u> and not be afraid of making mistakes. ('Linguistics')

A characteristic response to a suggestion on a 'Talk' page is

> Add what you deem appropriate. Let's see where that takes us. ('Accents')

'Let's see where it takes us' is an ideal comment for an undergraduate seminar or a research group discussion, but it may come as a surprise to people whose idea of knowledge is based on exams and television quizzes. Many people are unhappy with the idea that there will, inevitably, be inaccurate or poorly-phrased contributions to *Wikipedia*, because they are thinking of it as claiming the authority of a paper encyclopaedia (if only because of its name).

Like the other principles, Be Bold can be used aggressively. In an example discussed in Chapter 9, *Chris Q* settles the back and forth edit war on whether Manchester was the second or third city by saying he or she would 'Be bold' – and making it third. In 'Global Warming', *The Person Who Is Strange* defies most of the regular editors of the article and inserts a phrase saying that the idea that human activity is leading to climate change is just a theory. Be Bold was meant to open up debate, not to close it by fiat.

10.2 Civility

When one reads the kinds of abuse that editors hurl at each other in comments on talk pages ('CRANK', 'nut', 'Gestapo', and, as we have seen, 'atavistic traditionalist'), it may come as a surprise that another official *Wikipedia* principles is 'Civility'. The principle defined at length on WP:CIVILITY , and summarized at the top of 'Talk' pages: 'Be polite. Assume good faith. No personal attacks. Be welcoming.' So an administrator joining in a discussion of some edits questions the heading it has been given, 'Excessive hacking of page'.

> The title of this discussion – i.e., the reference to hacking – violates the the Wikipedia rule of assuming someone has good intentions. – <u>Alabamaboy</u>

There is a similar example in Chapter 9 when *JimWae* first suggests that the new contributor put their rant on the 'Talk' page, and only when it is reinstated twice in the article without discussion concludes 'guess it's just vandalism – not unfamiliarity with talk pages and encyclopedia'. There is a lot of 'please' and 'thank you' in these discussions, and not all the uses are ironic.

But there is more to politeness than 'please' and 'thank you'; Wikipedians use a wide range of devices to signal to mitigate threats to face (see Chapters 6 and 7 on politeness in blogs). Most of the devices are similar to those one sees in academic discourse, such as hedging (*I think, probably, sort of*) and concessions ('I agree that . . ., but . . .'). But there is also much more emphasis on interactional style in argument, as in apologies, questions and the use of discourse particles (*well*) and non-words (*uh huh, ahem*) normally found only in conversation.

As one might expect, there are many examples of hedging, features that weaken claims by adding modals, verbs of cognition or perception, or discourse markers to signal lack of complete commitment to the claim. After a criticism of an added bit in 'Vegetarianism', Guaka says 'So **I guess** this needs some rewriting . . . :)'. The next editor to comment is more direct, but also includes a hedge: '**I don't see** what the quoted passage has to do with vegetarianism in the first place (*Mkweise*)'. The negative and thus face-threatening statements hedged by introductions that suggest *Guaka*'s uncertainty (*I guess*) or the idea that this is possibly just the Mkweise's inability to make the connection (*I don't see*), not the objective lack of a connection of the added material to the topic. Modal adverbs (*possibly, probably, might*) can also hedge, as in *probably* in the next example:

> –Just for the record, absolute zero is **probably** unattainable (thanks to quantum mechanics).
> –Absolute zero IS unobtainable. This is a consequence of the third law of thermodynamics. (Lancaster University)

The *probably* in the first statement is does not necessarily show uncertainty; such hedges are often used by scientists to show conventional modesty in confronting another scientist. But the second poster doesn't think such hedging is appropriate for dismissing a statement that is obviously wrong, and actually heightens the categorical assertion. So there is a place for both politeness and a carefully targeted impoliteness. In the 'Shakespeare' Talk pages a rejection of a statement is qualified as 'it is hard to believe', but the following sentence draws the implication of this evidence more emphatically, in a categorical statement.

> So it is **hard to believe** the three men were part of a conspiracy to assert the falsehood of Shakespeare's authorship. No, the theory that Shakespeare didn't write most of the Shakespearean works doesn't hold water. ('Shakespeare')

The 'No' marks it as a direct, conversational response to the opponent, a device I will return to later.

The principles of Civility endorsed by *Wikipedia* explicitly call for apologies where one has offended someone:

> Oops
> I think I made an error and deleted a chunk of the page somehow. Would somebody please fix that? – unsigned ('Copyright')

But of course, an apology can be used for rhetorical purposes. We see that in an earlier example, criticizing a journal as a source for the 'Vaccination' article, beginning *'I'm sorry*, but the political agenda of JpandS is relevant . . .' The 'sorry' softens the criticism, but does not indicate that the critic is feeling any remorse. In the following examples, *MarkThomas*'s 'Sorry' is a preface to a direct accusation, and *dbasldon*'s 'Forgive me' is a preface to a statement about which he knows he is not mistaken.

> <u>Sorry Andy</u>, but you are misunderstanding what I'm saying, and **with respect to you**, **can I propose** you actually read my paragraph and not make unjustified statements about my lack of understanding of WP guidelines . . . – <u>MarkThomas</u> ('Shakespeare')

> **Forgive me** if i'm mistaken, but there hasn't been a NIST report released about the collapse of WTC 7 yet . . . –dbasldon ('7 World Trade Center')

The apologies may not be sincere, and may come across as ironic, but they still work to mitigate impolite acts because they are part of a rhetoric of addressing opponents directly rather than building a case against them indirectly. Academics can use apologies this way too, but may avoid them because they call attention to the personal nature of the interaction.

Questions can also be used sincerely and insincerely (see Chapters 6 and 7). Often they are (or may be) genuine requests for additional information.

> –Vegetarianism has strong links to many religious traditions, including Hinduism, Jainism, Buddhism, Taoism, and others.
> –**Taoism? Really?** I've never heard this. ('Vegetarianism')

But typically they are rhetorical questions intended to show up weaknesses in the opposing case.

> **is there any evidence** to back up your assertation that there are numerous reputable scholars that believe Oxford is the author? I think undue weight does apply to Oxford. ('Shakespeare')

Here the editor reveals their intention by going on to say that the principle of Undue Weight applies, that is, they presuppose a negative answer to the question of whether there is evidence.

Another familiar device of academic politeness is the concession (as we saw in Chapter 7). For instance, *Crum375* is explaining to an editor why they can't post their artwork on the page:

> **First, let me say that the fact that you are eager to help and improve WP is greatly appreciated by all of us**, so please don't be discouraged by anything I am about to say. **But** to contribute in a productive and useful way you have to understand what WP is about. Again, please read the various policies, e.g. WP:NOT , WP:OR and many more. ('Computed Tomography')

In the following example, the linguist says that technical terms are needed, but a gloss should be provided. The weight comes down on what follows the 'still'.

> But I agree that the vocabulary is necessarily technical. **Still**, accessibility is a worthwhile aim, and it's not too hard to produce glosses for most things that point the layman in the right direction, like: 'Homorganic consonants (consonants pronounced using the same parts of the mouth) . . .'. (Linguistics)

Concessions are at the heart of *Wikipedia* Civility, which envisions a kind of give and take, arriving at a consensus. But they are also rhetorical devices, like the hedges, questions and apologies, that show the writer is a rational, cooperative contributor to the shared project.

10.3 Conversational discourse markers

Wikipedians often use the language of conversations in their written contributions to 'Talk' pages, including discourse particles such as *well*, *umm* and *ahem*. This register may serve a politeness function, marking the response as casual, offhand, not claiming the authority of a full written case. And it marks the response as linked directly to the previous comment.

> –Name an instance where these so-called 'real' boundaries changed, and you accept both the situation before and that change as legitimate. – Morwen
> **–Hmmm** . . . For example, I accept that, as of 1133, Carlisle ceased to be part of Durham 80.255 ('Counties')
>
> –Accents and dialects vary more widely within the U.K. itself than they do in other parts of the world owing to the longer history of the language within the countries of the U.K. [Derek Ross]
> **–Um,** perhaps in the English language, but hardly true of all countries? – Zoe ('Accents')

[after claim that 'The Tempest could not have been written by Shakespeare']
–**Ahem.** In the Signet Classic Shakespeare (edited by Sylvan Barnet of Tufts University), in several volumes weight is given to the theory that Fletcher wrote part of several 'Shakespearean' plays, including The Two Noble Kinsmen and Henry VIII. This makes sense to me, as parts of these plays are in Fletcher's distinct style . . . – <u>Grantsky</u> ('Shakespeare')

[after an edit saying Manchester was 'one of the first' industrial cities]
–**Naah**, Manchester really is regarded as the first industrial city. Go to google scholar and enter <u>'first industrial city'</u> and see what you get . . . <u>Mr Stephen</u>

In the first example, *80.255* is responding to a direct personal challenge from *Morwen*, and signals that he is thinking it over. In the second, *Zoe* is signalling doubt at the breadth of the statement, and asks a question (instead of asserting that *Derek Ross* is wrong. In the third example, *Grantsky* precedes a dismissal of the claim that Shakespeare did not write *The Tempest* with throat-clearing 'ahem', and then a concession that they are willing to grant doubts about other late plays. And in the fourth, *Mr Stephen* is returning to a familiar argument, with a conversational 'Naah' rather than a more formal 'No' marking his emphatic rejection of the edit.

Such devices work, I think, by signalling a shift to a less formal register, taking on the style of a conversation rather than a treatise. This is particularly clear with a particle that one seldom sees in writing, *pfft*, which is apparently imitating the dismissive sound of breath escaping sharply through one's teeth:

–No, it is wrong for an encyclopedic entry to have such generalizations as 'goths take it', not in those exact words but that is basically what it would be saying and this can not be proven as fact, same with housewifes and yuppies as you so put it.
–Pfft. Goths are given <u>zoloft</u> on sight where I live . . . <u>144.131.139.111</u> ('Fluoxetine')

I see that in all the Wikipedia Talk pages 30 instances of *pffft* (with three fs) and 140 of *pfft* (I wouldn't care to explain the functional difference between the two spellings). The same sort of shift to spoken register occurs in blogs, when critical comments on posts leave in the typos and marks of informality that show this to be an offhand response, not a carefully drafted attack.

Conversational devices and politeness devices are part of an interpersonal rhetoric that depersonalizes conflicts on *Wikipedia* and enables

155

the editing of an article to continue, instead of falling into a cycle of reverts and name-calling. It shows new participants what the community takes as normal behaviour, more subtly than by referring them to WP:CIVILITY. And such behaviour also shows other readers of the controversy on the Talk page that one is a rational and experienced editor (unlike, it might be suggested, one's opponent). All this contributes to the sense of a Community of Practice, a group of people sharing a project, its codes, roles and communication system (Wenger 1998).

10.4 Consensus, community and anger

Collaboration is essential to Wikipedia. Individuals may add statements to the pages (as we saw in Chapter 9), but it takes a collaborative effort to link the statements, make them relevant, check them, and if necessary defend them. A statement in a popular *Wikipedia* article only persists by being when it is accepted, re-used, and probably modified by other editors. The consensus that results is rather tenuous, so it is no surprise that it is a mystery to occasional Wikipedia editors who want a poll or vote. It is ideally the result of a kind of *deliberative democracy* (for this term, see 'What I read'), the result of collective discussion and rational persuasion, not just the aggregation of individual opinions.

> *New users* who are not yet familiar with consensus should realize that a poll (if one is even held) is often more likely to be the start of a discussion than it is to be the end of one. The outcome may be decided *during discussion.* . . Wikipedia's decisions are not based on the number of people who showed up and voted a particular way on a particular day; they are based on a system of good reasons. ('WP: Consensus')

The continuation of this work depends on a shared sense of belonging to a project. Editors repeatedly refer to and disagree about what they see as the purpose of an encyclopaedia.

> We can rephrase it to 'critics raise the question' if you feel better about it, but I think it is perfectly in keeping with an encyclopedia to raise questions. – Leifern ('Vaccines')

> WP is an *encyclopedia* – that means it is essentially a summary of notable work that has been published and thereby became notable elsewhere. ('Computed Tomography')

> No, it is wrong for an encyclopedic entry to have such generalizations as 'goths take it', not in those exact words but that is basically what it would be saying and this can not be proven as fact ('Fluoxetine')

The slogan to the top right of this page is 'The free Encylopedia', would such an event [the Goerge Fox 6] really be in the free encyclopedia? ('Lancaster University')

I do not see how as a people's encyclopedia one can speak so definitively on something that is more grounded on emotion than fact. – Knowledgebycoop ('7 World Trade Center')

Perhaps it was a mistake to use the 'pedia' suffix that gave users a somewhat misleading sense of what *Wikipedia* could be (see Chapter 2). But it has also held up an ideal on which these editors implicitly draw, to include or exclude statements.

Consensus is essential to *Wikipedia*. There is even an essay (not a principle) entitled 'WikiLove' (with which one editor has, inevitably, disagreed: 'I prefer coolheaded, courteous bluntness to cloying, sugary affectation'). So why is it always threatened by name-calling, ALL-CAPITALIZING, exclamation-point-stabbing rage? How can users become so angry about the population of Manchester or the existence of an eighteenth-century writer like Mary Wollstonecraft? It may be that there is a fundamental tension in *Wikipedia* between private and public conceptions of knowledge. Again, and again, editors accuse others of shutting them up, not letting them have their opinions, not putting their view in the lead, being Nazis or Stalinists. They are assuming a model of knowledge like that in the blogosphere, in which everyone is entitled to say what they want, and the mechanisms of popularity and links will sort it out. *Wikipedia* assumes an opposing conception of knowledge as inherently public, a group project. Usually, as we have seen, arguments can be settled, at least for the time being. But when they can't be, the free thinker / conspiracy theorist / vandal, or the follower / consensus-oriented / scholar stalk off, thinking not just that they have been mistreated, but that the ideal of *Wikipedia* has been betrayed.

10.5 What I did

I chose the articles for these chapters to focus on revisions and in the mediation of conflicts between editors. For the first purpose, I looked at articles that had achieved 'Featured Article' status (marked here with *), and chose two of them for closer analysis in Chapter 9. For the second, I looked at articles from *Wikipedia*'s 'List of Controversial Articles' (marked with **). I also looked at some other topics with local connections, or on topics in the news, or on topics in my academic field, so that I would know something about the content.

- Cloning**
- Copyright

- Fluoxetine
- Global Warming**
- Historical Counties of England**
- Intelligence
- Lancaster University
- Lancaster Royal Grammar School
- Linguistics
- Manchester*
- Mary Wollstonecraft*
- Madeleine McCann
- Regional Accents of English
- Seattle, Washington*
- 7 World Trade Center* and **
- Silesia**
- Travelling Salesman Problem
- Vaccine controversy**
- Vegetarianism**
- William Shakespeare Authorship* and **

I put the the most recent 5,000 words from the 'Talk' page of each of these articles in rtf form into Atlas ti so that I could code the kinds of rhetoric across all the examples (You could do the same kind of coding just by marking a printout with codes). I arrived at these codes (more or less my headings in these chapters) by starting with a general list of Wikipedia principles and politeness strategies, and modified the list as I went along (for instance, I hadn't expected the conversational particles such as 'oh' and sound effects such as 'pfft').

10.6 What I read

In addition to the readings on *Wikipedia* in Chapter 9, I touch on three broader concepts in this chapter. One is the system of rewards and motivations for participating in a shared project. Bruns comments on personal merit and rewards in all systems of what he calls *produsage* (2008: 29), and Shirky has a chapter on how it works in *Wikipedia* (2008: Chapter 5); Baker gives a nice narrative of his own motivations (Baker 2008). A concern with reputation is a defining feature of the new forms of interaction grouped as 'Web 2.0', such as *Wikipedia*, *Flickr* and *Second Life* (Lankshear and Knobel 2006).

Another central concept is *Community of Practice*, an idea arising from the work of Jean Lave and Etienne Wenger, on how people can learn by being participants in a shared project (Wenger 1998; see also Barton and Tusting 2005). *Wikipedia* is such a project; in particular, it has what Wenger calls mutual engagement (anyone can edit), a joint enterprise (of making an article), a shared repertoire of forms (such as Talk pages and User pages) and a process of learning by people at the boundaries of the project ('Don't bite the newbies').

I also mention the idea of *deliberative democracy*. This is a view of democracy as resulting from rational discussion among all participants, not just from the aggregation of the votes of individuals (Dryzek 1990; Benhabib 1996; Elster 1998; Dryzek 2000; Gutman and Thompson 2004). There is a reasonably good introduction (as of May 2008) in *Wikipedia*'s article 'Deliberative Democracy'.

A note on studying the language of blogs and wikis

Blogs make for appealing projects for students: the subject matter can be interesting, the styles are lively and personal, and the data couldn't be easier to collect (no taping and transcription). But from my experience with BA and MA students, there are some practical problems to consider, and these practical problems raise some interesting issues for discourse analysis in general.

Here are some topics of studies by students at my university.

- Comparing news blogs to news reports – e.g., Iraq, Katrina, a political demonstration
- Uses of narrative (tense, evaluation, reported speech) in personal diaries – e.g., *Bitch PhD*, *Dooce*
- Attempts of politicians to find an ethos for blogging, *Facebook*, and other online forms of presence – e.g., US Presidential candidates
- Uses of informality, for instance colloquialisms and typos in comments
- Community building (solidarity, banter, shared assumptions) – e.g., anorexics, soldiers, fans of a football team
- Evaluative language in specialist blogs – e.g., cookery blogs
- Language choice and code-switching (no longer English domination)

There are also language issues to study in other recent innovations in Web 2.0, such as in the comments on YouTube and on photo sharing sites, the wall on Facebook, the use of a short text saying what you are doing on Twitter.

Problems and choices

Blogs provide a vast source of data already in electronic form, so it is easy to download material, save it as text, and use concordancing tools to find keywords and collocations. But there are some theoretically interesting practical problems:

- As we have seen in my studies, blogs are hard to sample. There is no list of the whole blogosphere, no 'representative sample' from that list, so one usually has to explain a theoretically motivated sample, as I did. One can choose the most popular, or blogs linked to each other, or blogs in some unusual form or style, or blogs on a topic.

- Students always ask how much text they need, and there is no right answer. For my chapters, I tended to go for about 10,000 words from each of the blogs I was using. If I wanted to make a statistical argument contrasting blogs and posts, or one kind of blog and another, I would need a much larger sample. These corpora are easy enough to collect, just cut and paste, but students are likely to blanch at the thought of analysing qualitatively 100,000 words, the length of an academic monograph.

- Students have raised the issue of just what they should cut and paste. It can be hard to collect the comments as well as the posts, because one usually has to follow the permanent links for each post, but I have shown in Chapters 6 that they can be very different kinds of texts (for instance, one is likely to find a lot more evaluative comments in posts, and more contrastive statements highlighting the place of the writer). If one followed up trackbacks and links, one would be in for a couple days of copying and pasting, and a lot of hard choices, rather than just an hour or two.

- If you want the whole text, with the visuals and layout, consider using a site for that purpose, such as HTTrack off-line browser http://www.httrack.com/.

- I copy all my texts as rtf files into qualitative analysis software, in my case Atlas-ti. One nice effect of this translation is that the links show up with the URLs, so I can tell what they are linking to. It looks messy, but it makes some kinds of analysis easier. Others analyse the texts with corpus software such as Wordsmith. For that, one needs text-only format.

- When I say in the chapters that I coded my texts, I mean I started with a list of categories, and marked every time an example of one of these categories occurred. The list evolved as I coded with some categories collapsing, and some added. For instance, the categories for Chapter 4 began with a checklist of linguistic devices I expected, such as deictic expressions. I found that prepositional phrases, which were on my list, didn't usually have this function. But other devices did have this function, such as the reference to local places, and the use of photographs. This kind of revision of categories comes from Grounded Theory, an approach that encourages researchers to move from the specifics of their data to increasingly general theoretical accounts.

161

Ethics, consent and ownership

When I was about halfway through this book, a questioner at a conference raised the ethical issues around collecting and using this kind of data. I could see there would be issues of consent and confidentiality if I used blogs from a support network for a medical condition, or blogs meant to be read only by family and friends. But I have chosen only what I consider to be public blogs on public issues, where the authors obviously expected to have their words read by the widest possible audience; all are quoted frequently by other bloggers, and nearly all of them have had some comment and quotation in mainstream media. There are still issues of reproducing the words of bloggers, because they retain copyright, or some form of creative commons ownership of their work. So I have requested permission from all the frequently quoted bloggers in this book who provided some form of contact; most didn't respond but the few that did gave permission.

A blog as the coursework?

All this so far is about using blogs as data for a conventional coursework essay. What about using a blog as the form of the essay, tracing the development of one's ideas over time? Despite encouragement, I have not gotten my students to write blogs instead of conventional coursework essays. Other teachers may have been more successful (see Bruns and Jacobs (2006)). I'm not too disappointed, because I can see some pitfalls for all but the most academically adept and reflexive students. In my own blogging, I have felt a tension between the process and the finished work, and I could be accused of not really using the potential of the web form, for instance in links. As you might expect, I usually write up a mini-essay and post it, and it shows. Even cleverer and more experienced academic bloggers tend to have texts that break down into little posts, and I'm not sure it would be fair to compare such bitty texts to the sustained argument of the ideal dissertation. There are also problems of voice. I feel pompous if I use my academic voice on my blog, but the flip and ironic colloquial tone of blogs may serve to cover vagueness and conventionality. Finally, there is the question of the firewall. If the blogs are public, they are open to vandalism and trolls and spam and all sorts of stuff – not what one wants in a high-stakes piece of coursework. But if they are behind the university firewall, inaccessible to the public, they aren't really blogs, and they will miss those sudden surprising contacts that I have gotten even in my little blog. In looking for practical resolutions to these problems, I keep checking out the excellent research blogs by PhD students. They find ways of mixing the personal and the intellectual that might serve as better models for students than either the heavy pedagogical tone of my blog, or the flippant superficiality and rants of some of the more popular blogs. And of course *Language Log*, often quoted in these pages, shows what a group can do with more time, care and wit (and wider knowledge of linguistics too).

More resources

As I have worked on this book, I have found that, not surprisingly, many of the most useful resources are online. Some of the main researchers on blogs have pages on blogs that give lots of papers; these are particularly useful in starting students off on their reading. I have also listed some web resources, such as *Technorati*, the search engine and ranking tool, and *Data-Mining*, which experiments with visualizations. See my own blog for updates in the first year after this book.

- My blog: http://thelanguageofblogs.typepad.com/
- Technorati – the most-used search engine for blogs – http://www.technorati.com/
- Global Voices – a carefully edited directory translating and summarizing blogs from around the world – a good source for finding well-written blogs that give a non-US perspective – http://www.globalvoicesonline.org/
- Data Mining: Text Mining, Visualization and Social Media – Useful visualizations of the blogosphere by a Microsoft researcher http://datamining.typepad.com/data_mining/graphs/index.html
- Blog Herald – news on blogs, mostly business-related – http://www.blogherald.com/
- The Sum of My Parts – the home page of Stephanie Hendricks, who is completing a PhD on blogs – http://www.sumofmyparts.org/blog/
- Rebecca's Pocket – Rebecca Blood's blog links to lots of commentary on blogs – http://www.rebeccablood.net/
- Jill Walker – another academic blog by a pioneer of blogging – http://jilltxt.net/
- On the Media – the weekly WNYC (Public Broadcasting System) radio programme regularly covers blogs and new media, and has podcasts and transcripts – http://www.onthemedia.org/
- Journal of Computer-Mediated Communication – currently the best source of academic articles on blogs – http://jcmc.indiana.edu/

Glossary

These definitions are to help you understand how I use the terms in this book. For more precise and extensive definitions, see Biber et al. (1999) for grammatical terms, or the 'Glossary' of the *Internet Grammar of English* from University College London, at http://www.ucl.ac.uk/internet-grammar/frames/glossary.htm. For rhetorical terms, see Lanham (1968). *Wikipedia* is pretty good for most of the media terms on this list.

Address – In this book, the act of naming or indicating someone specific as the recipient of one's message. Of course that named person or group may not be the only recipient, or even the main recipient, for instance when one makes an aside to one person in a blog read by thousands, or when one writes an 'open letter' to a politician unlikely to read it (Chapter 6).

Adverbial – A part of a sentence (the other parts are subject, predicate, object and complement) that gives the circumstances or manner of the main part of the clause, or a stance on it. It can be a word, phrase or clause. One test is that it can usually be moved to several different places in the sentence (Chapter 7).

Affordance – James Gibson's term for the way we perceive elements of the environment, such as a new technology, in terms of how we might use them (Chapter 3).

Animator – In Erving Goffman's analysis of footing, the Animator is the person who does the speaking or writing down of the words, who is not necessarily the same one who thought of the words or the person in whose name they are spoken or written (Chapter 6).

Aspect – The tense of a verb tells us whether the action took place in the past or present; aspect tells whether the action is or was complete or incomplete, for instance continuous aspect *he is writing* or prefect aspect *he had written* (Chapter 5).

Author – In Erving Goffman's analysis of footing, the Author is the person who thought of the words, not necessarily the same one who then speaks or writes them down (Chapter 6).

Bystander – In Erving Goffman's analysis of footing, participants who are not the addressed audience, but whose presence is perceivable by the participants, for instance lurkers who might read a blog that is mainly intended for family and friends, or other readers of an exchange between two Wikipedians on a 'Talk' page (Chapter 6).

Clause – A complete unit with (usually) a subject and predicate; it can be either independent, or dependent on another clause (Chapter 7).

Complement clause – A clause that completes the verb or adjective, for instance after *I think that . . .* (Chapter 7).

Cooperative Principle – The basis of H. Paul Grice's approach to conversation, the assumption that participants in talk (or in other shared activities) assume that the other person will say things that are true, sufficient, relevant and clear (Chapters 3 and 6).

Creative Commons – An organization that provides licences by which people can share and develop work, as an alternative to copyright; these licences allow others to re-use them, retaining only specific stated rights, such as the right to be attributed with creation of the work (Chapter 9).

Deduction – Reasoning from general truths to specific cases; for instance if it is true that all Americans talk too much, and Greg is an American, then it is true that Greg talks too much (Chapter 8).

Defeasibility – The property of some statements that they can be undone without logical contradiction. For instance, implicatures are defeasible (Chapter 6).

Deixis – 'Pointing words' that take their meaning from the specific situation of the speaker/writer and hearer/reader, such as *here* and *there*, *now* and *then* (Chapters 4 and 5).

Deontic modality – auxiliary verbs that mark necessity or obligation, such as *must, should, ought to* (Chapter 7).

Dynamic modality – auxiliary verbs that mark ability or permission, such as *can* or *able to, have to* (Chapter 7).

Epistemic modality – auxiliary verbs that mark degrees of certainty or possibility, such as *may* and *might* (Chapter 8).

Face – Erving Goffman's term for what it is we protect in our desire to be seen in a good light, a sense similar to that the word has in *losing face* or *saving face*. In Brown and Levinson's conception, linguistic politeness is a way of mitigating threats to the face of the other or of the speaker (Chapter 6).

Flout – Breaking one of Grice's maxims in a way that signals to the hearer that the speaker intends for it to be obvious that the maxim is broken, so that the hearer draws an implicature (Chapters 3 and 6). For instance, saying 'And I am Conan the Barbarian' when one is not, and when the reader knows full well that one is not, could generate the implicature that if this statement is obviously wrong, the statement to which it is responding is also obviously wrong.

Genre – A standardized form of text for standardized social functions, such as a job application letter, a textbook or (arguably) a blog (Chapter 2).

Hedge – Any term or phrase that is used to weaken or boost the speaker's or writer's commitment to a statement, for instance '*I think* that' or '*Maybe* you need to think about that'. Hedges are often used for purposes of politeness, to mitigate potential face threatening acts (Chapter 6).

HTML – HyperText Mark-up Language, the set of codes used for web pages that enables a text to be read in the same way by different browsers on different computers, and that enables a text to embed links to other texts (Chapters 2 and 8).

Implicature – A further proposition, attitude or piece of information conveyed when a speaker flouts one of Grice's maxims (Chapters 3 and 6).

Induction – Reasoning from what is observed of specific cases to the truth of a more general proposition. For instance, if one observes that Greg is American and talks too much, and you meet another American who talks too much, you might conclude all Americans talk too much. Of course this may not be true; the next American you meet might be rather quiet (Chapter 8).

Intertextuality – An element of one text that takes its meaning from a reference to another text, for instance by quoting, echoing or linking (Chapter 3).

Metaphor – A figure of speech in which one thing is talked about in terms of another ('love is a rose') (Chapter 6).

Modality – The marking of the speaker's attitude towards a statement, usually through a closed set of auxiliary verbs (as in my definitions above), but also, more widely, through modal nouns, adjectives and adverbs that do similar work (Chapter 7).

Narrowcast – By contrast to broadcast media (radio and television), a narrowcast medium addresses a specific and perhaps very small audience (for instance a mailing list, or a blog about bread baking) (see Chapter 6).

Nominalization – The process of making an action that might usually be represented by a verb, or quality that usually might be represented by an adjective, into a noun. Often (but not always) it is signalled by the *-ation* ending. For instance, the noun *wiki* can be made into the verb *wikify*, meaning to add the wiki markup to the text so that the references work in a consistent way. Then in nominalization, the verb *wikify* can be made into *wikification*, the process of adding markup (Chapter 7).

Overhearer – In Erving Goffman's analysis of footing, a participant who has accidentally come across a message for which they are not the intended recipient. If they deliberately set up a situation in which they get a message not intended for them, Goffman calls them 'eavesdroppers' (Chapter 6).

Phrase – A group of words that go together as a unit of a clause. For instance a noun phrase includes a noun and any adjectives, determiners and propositional phrases that go with it, and it can fill the same sorts of slots in a clause as a single-word noun (Chapter 7).

Politeness – In this book, the use of linguistic devices to mitigate a face threatening act, such as a criticism or a directive, for instance by making a statement impersonal, or using hedges to soften it (Chapter 6).

Principal – In Erving Goffman's analysis of footing, the person or entity in whose name words are uttered. For instance, a spokesperson may utter words, but they are attributed to the official or organization. I suspect that most dog blogs are written by the owner of the dog; the dog is the principal, the owner is the author and animator (Chapter 6).

Produsage – The term coined by Axel Bruns to refer to the way users become producers of texts in Web 2.0 sites such as blogs, Flickr and YouTube; that is, you can consume the texts you find there, add value to them by adding tags or comments, or produce your own (Chapters 2 and 8).

Ratified participant – In Erving Goffman's analysis of footing, the person or group presented as the audience for an utterance. For instance, in a lecture, the teacher and all the students are ratified participants in the event, whether the students are listening or not, and someone visiting to observe the teaching is a bystander (Chapter 6).

Reported speech – The term I am using for all forms of direct and indirect quotation, reference to, or re-use of words or thoughts from another context. Semino and Short (2004) call it 'Speech, Thought, and Writing Presentation', arguing that is isn't necessarily reported (it might be made up or hypothetical) and it isn't necessarily speech (Chapter 7).

Stance – The term used by Biber et al. (1999) for all ways of marking the speaker's or writer's attitude towards or commitment to their statements. In this book I focus on one specific category, in which the writer marks an attitude towards a separate proposition, for instance by making it a complement after *I think* (Chapter 7).

Synecdoche – A figure of speech in which a part stands for the whole, for instance 'all hands' to mean 'all workers' (Chapter 3).

Tense – The marking of a verb to indicate a time of the action in relation to the present, for instance present, past and pluperfect (Chapter 5).

Text – A groups of signs that go together to form a coherent whole. So, for instance, a blog post is a text, and usually has many cohesive links to suggest the words go together, while the list of results from a search engine, though they may all be about the same thing, is not read as a text (Chapter 3).

Violation – Breaking one of Grice's maxims in a way that is not apparent to the listener, for instance breaking the maxim of quality by lying. Violations do not generate implicatures; flouts do (Chapters 3 and 6).

Web 2.0 – Tim O'Reilly's (2005) term for a stage of development of the internet marked by the growth of applications that are web-based (rather than in one's own computer), that work across platforms, and that harness the contributions of users to produce additional value (see http://www.oreillynet.com/pub/a/oreilly/tim/news/2005/09/30/what-is-web-20.html). Examples include blogs, *Wikipedia*, *Flickr*, *YouTube*, *Facebook* and *Second Life* (Chapter 2).

Widget – A bit of code one can embed in an HTML page, leading to an application provided elsewhere, for instance to count the visitors to one's site, give the weather, or play a YouTube video. The term arises from an earlier, partly joking, generalized term for a product, as in this 1971 use in the Hartford *Courant* (which I found via Google News): 'Suppose you were an honest, God-fearing manufacturer of say, widgets and, as such, part of the mythical widget industry doing a multi-billion dollar business . . .' (Chapter 3).

WTF – 'What The Fuck', an expression of astonishment at some news (sometimes cleaned up so that it is said to stand for 'Where's the Fire'), (Used as an example of an insider acronym in Chapter 6).

Blog addresses

These are the URLs and the dates sampled, so that readers can look up the full texts if they wish. My aim was to get roughly the same number of words for each blog in each period sampled, so the number of days covered varies, with few days (or one) for bloggers that post a lot, and many days for bloggers with infrequent posts. Bloggers often changed their web hosts over the course of the study (e.g., *India Uncut*, *Israeli-Mom*, *Cosmic Variance*, *Language Log*), but in each case the old address has a link to the new one, and the new address has archives.

101 Cookbooks http://www.101cookbooks.com/
22 April–3 May 2007; 17 July–26 August 2007; 14–19 November 2007;
   15–22 May 2008

Baghdad Burning http://riverbendblog.blogspot.com/
2 May–31 May 2006 (stopped in 2007)

Bitch PhD http://bitchphd.blogspot.com/
27 April–7 May 2007; 24–27 August 2007; 19–21 November 2007;
   19–23 May 2008

BlackProf http://blackprof.com/
3–8 May 2007; 12–20 May 2008

BoingBoing http://www.boingboing.net/
1 June 2006; 6–7 May 2007; 26 May 2008

Chocolate & Zucchini http://chocolateandzucchini.com/
5 April–1 May 2007

Climb to the Stars – Stephanie Booth http://climbtothestars.org/
11–28 August 2007; 12–21 November 2007

Cosmic Variance http://cosmicvariance.com/
29 May–1 June 2006; 30 April–6 May 2007; 21–26 May 2008

Dr Dave's Blog http://unknowngenius.com/blog/
15–19 April 2007; 5 February–26 May 2008;

Dooce http://www.dooce.com/
3–28 August 2007; 6–27 November 2007; 23 April–26 May 2008

Global Voices Online – Bob Chen http://globalvoicesonline.org/
   author/ bob-chen/
19–26 May 2008

Going Underground's Blog http://london-underground.blogspot.com/
25 April–7 May 2007; 21–31 August 2007; 2–21 November 2007; 7–28
   May 2008

India Uncut – published by Amit Varma http://indiauncut.com/
29 May–1 June 2006; 28 April–4 May 2007; 23–28 August 2007; 14–22
   November 2007; 4–26 May 2008

Instapundit http://www.instapundit.com/
1 June 2006; 7 May 2007; 29–30 August 2007; 21 November 2007;
   21–26 May 2008

Israeli Mom http://www.israelimom.org/
6 March–3 June 2008

Language Log http://languagelog.ldc.upenn.edu/nll/
26–28 August 2007; 20–21 November 2007; 25–27 May 2008

My Mom's Blog by Thoroughly Modern Millie http://www.
   mymomsblog.blogspot.com/
16 March–31 May 2008

Raising Yousuf, Unplugged http://a-mother-from-gaza.blogspot.com/
25 July–27 August 2007; 19 September–13 November 2007;
   23 March–19 May 2008

Sepia Mutiny http://www.sepiamutiny.com/sepia/
27 August 2007; 21 November 2007

West End Whingers http://westendwhingers.wordpress.com/
13–31 May 2008

Jonathan Edelstein stopped publishing *HeadHeeb* in 2007, and there is
no longer an archive of it on blogmosis.com. I used data from 29 May to
1 June 2006 and 3–7 May 2007.

170

References

Abercrombie, N. and B. Longhurst (1998). *Audiences: A Sociological Theory of Performance and Imagination.* London, Sage.

Adam, B. (1998). *Timescapes of Modernity: The Environment and Invisible Hazards.* London, Routledge.

Alasuutari, P., Ed. (1999). *Rethinking the Media Audience.* London, Sage.

Allan, S. (2006). *Online News: Journalism and the Internet.* Maidenhead, UK, Open University Press.

Augé, M. (1995). *Non-places: An Introduction to the Anthropology of Supermodernity.* London, Verso.

Bhatia, V. (2004). *Worlds of Written Discourse: A Genre-based View.* London, Continuum.

Baker, N. (2008). The charms of Wikipedia. *New York Review of Books* **55**(4): 6–10.

Baker, S. and H. Green (2008). Beyond blogs: What business needs to know. *Business Week.* 22 May. http://www.businessweek.com/magazine/content/08_22/b4086044617865.htm

Barton, D. and K. Tusting, Eds (2005). *Beyond Communities of Practice.* Cambridge, Cambridge University Press.

Basso, K. H. (1996). Wisdom sits in places: Notes on a Western Apache landscape. *Senses of Place.* K. H. Basso. Santa Fe, NM, School of American Research Press: 53–90.

Bazerman, C. (1988). *Shaping Written Knowledge: The Genre and Activity of the Experimental Article in Science.* Madison, WI, University of Wisconsin Press.

Benhabib, S., Ed. (1996). *Democracy and Difference: Contesting the Boundaries of the Political.* Princeton, NJ, Princeton University Press.

Berkenkotter, C. and T. Huckin (1995). *Genre Knowledge in Disciplinary Communication.* Hillsdale, NJ, Erlbaum.

Biber, D. and E. Finegan (1989). Styles of stance in English: Lexical and grammatical marking of evidentiality and affect. *Text* **9**(1): 93–124.

Biber, D., S. Johansson, G. Leech, S. Conrad and E. Finegan (1999). *Longman Grammar of Spoken and Written English.* London, Longman.

Billig, M. (1995). *Banal Nationalism.* London, Sage.

Blood, R. (2002a). Introduction. *We've Got Blog.* J. Rodzvilla. Cambridge, Perseus Publishing: ix–xiii.

—(2002b). *The Weblog Handbook: Practical Advice on Creating and Maintaining Your Blog.* Cambridge, MA, Perseus.

—(2002c). Weblogs: A history and perspective. *We've Got Blog*. J. Rodzvilla. Cambridge, MA, Perseus Publishing: 7–16.

Boardman, M. (2005). *The Language of Websites*. London, Routledge.

Brooker, W. and D. Jermyn (2003). *The Audience Studies Reader*. London, Routledge.

Broughton, J. (2008). *Wikipedia: The Missing Manual*. Sebastopol, CA, O'Reilly Media.

Brown, P. and S. Levinson (1987). *Politeness: Some Universals in Language Use*. Cambridge, Cambridge University Press.

Bruns, A. (2008). *Blogs, Wikipedia, Second Life, and Beyond*. New York, Peter Lang.

Bruns, A. and J. Jacobs, Eds (2006). *Uses of Blogs*. New York, Peter Lang.

Bryant, S., A. Forte and A. Bruckman (2005). Becoming Wikipedian: Transformation of participation in a collaborative online encyclopedia. Group '05. www.cc.gatech.edu/~asb/papers/bryant-forte-bruckman-group05.pdf

Carter, R. (2004). *Language and Creativity: The Art of Common Talk*. London, Routledge.

Chafe, W. (1986). Evidentiality in English conversation and academic writing. *Evidentiality: The Linguistic Coding of Epistemology*. W. Chafe and J. Nichols. Norwood, NJ, Ablex: 261–272.

Chafe, W. L. (1994). *Discourse, Consciousness, and Time: The Flow and Displacement of Conscious Experience in Speaking and Writing*. Chicago, University of Chicago Press.

Channell, J. (1994). *Vague Language*. Oxford, Oxford University Press.

Conrad, S. and D. Biber (2000). Adverbial marking of stance in speech and writing. *Evaluation in text*. S. Hunston and G. Thompson. Oxford, Oxford University Press: 56–73.

Crystal, D. (2001). *Language and the Internet*. Cambridge, UK, Cambridge University Press.

—(2007). On not being a speech therapist. *DCBlog*.

Culpeper, J. (1996). Towards an anatomy of impoliteness. *Journal of Pragmatics* **25**: 349–367.

de Moor, A. and L. Efimova (2004). An argumentation analysis of weblog conversations. Proceedings of the 9th International Conference on the Language-Action Perspective in Communication Modelling, New Brunswick, NJ. https://doc.telin.nl/dscgi/ds.py/Get/File-41656/lap2004_demoor_efimova.pdf

Dixon, J. and K. Durrheim (2000). Displacing place-identity: A discursive approach to locating self and other. *British Journal of Social Psychology* **39**: 27–44.

Doctorow, C., R. Dornfest, J. S. Johnson, S. Powers, B. Trott and M. G. Trott (2002). *Essential Blogging*. Sebastopol, CA, O'Reilly & Associates.

Dryzek, J. S. (2000). *Deliberative Democracy and Beyond: Liberals, Critics, Contestations*. Oxford, Oxford University Press.

Dryzek, M. (1990). *Discursive Democracy: Politics, Policy, and Political science*. Cambridge, Cambridge University Press.

172

Eggins, S. and D. Slade (1997). *Analysing Casual Conversation*. London, Cassell.

Elster, J., Ed. (1998). *Deliberative Democracy*. Cambridge, Cambridge University Press.

Emigh, W. and S. Herring (2005). Collaborative authoring on the web: A genre analysis of two on-line encyclopedias. HICSS-38, IEEE Press.

Englebretson, R., Ed. (2007). *Stance-taking in Interaction*. Amsterdam, Jonn Benjamins.

Fairclough, N. (1989). *Language and Power*. Harlow, Longman.

—(2003). *Analysing Discourse: Text Analysis for Social Research*. London, Routledge.

Georgakopoulou, A. (2006). The other side of the story: Towards a narrative analysis of narratives-in-interaction. *Discourse Studies* **8**(2): 235–257.

—(2007). *Small Stories, Interaction, and Identities*. Amsterdam, John Benjamins.

Gibson, J. J. (1977). The theory of affordances. *Perceiving, Acting, and Knowing: Toward an Ecological Psychology*. R. Shaw and J. Bransford. Hillsdale, NJ, Lawrence Erlbaum: 67–82.

Gillmor, D. (2004). *We the Media*. Sebastapol, CA, O'Reilly Media.

Gitlin, T. (1998). Public sphere or public sphericules? *Media, Ritual, and Identity*. T. Liebes and J. Curran. London, Routledge: 168–174.

Goffman, E. (1974). *Frame Analysis: An Essay on the Organization of Experience*. New York, Harper & Row.

—(1981). *Forms of Talk*. Oxford, Basil Blackwell.

Grice, P. (1989). *Studies in the Way of Words*. Cambridge, MA, Harvard University Press.

Gurak, L. J., S. Antonijevic, L. Johnson, C. Ratliff and J. Reyman, Eds (2004). *Into the Blogosphere: Rhetoric, Community, and Culture of Weblogs*. http://blog.lib.umn.edu/blogosphere/

Gutman, A. and D. Thompson (2004). *Why Deliberative Democracy?* Princeton, Princeton University Press.

Halliday, M. A. K. (1985). *An Introduction to Functional Grammar*. London, Edward Arnold.

Herring, S. C. and J. C. Paolillo (2006). Gender and genre variation in weblogs. *Journal of Sociolinguistics* **10**(4): 439–459.

Herring, S. C., I. Kouper, J. C. Paolillo, L. A. Scheidt, M. Tyworth, P. Welsch, E. Wright and N. Yu (2005). Conversations in the blogosphere: An analysis 'from the bottom up'. Proceedings of the Thirty-Eighth Hawai'i International Conference on System Sciences (HICSS-38), IEEE. http://ella.slis.indiana.edu/~herring/blogconv.pdf

Herring, S. C., L. A. Scheidt, S. Bonus and E. Wright (2004). Bridging the gap: A genre analysis of weblogs. Proceedings of the 37th Hawai'i International Conference on System Sciences (HICSS-37), IEEE. http://csdl.computer.org/comp/proceedings/hicss/2004/2056/04/205640101b.pdf

Hewitt, H. (2005). *Blog: Understanding the Information Revolution that's Changing Your World*. Nashville, TN, Nelson Books.

Hoey, M. (2001). *Textual Interaction*. London, Routledge.

Hunston, S. and G. Thompson (2000). *Evaluation in Text: Authorial Stance and the Construction of Discourse*. Oxford, Oxford University Press.

Hutchby, I. (2001). Texts, technology, and affordances. *Sociology-the Journal of the British Sociological Association* **35**: 441–456.

Hyland, K. (1998). *Hedging in Scientific Research Articles.* Amsterdam, John Benjamins.

Ingold, T. (2000). *The Perception of the Environment: Essays in Livelihood, Dwelling, and Skill.* London, Routledge.

Johnstone, B. (1990). *Stories, Community, and Place: Narratives from Middle America.* Bloomington, IN, Indiana University Press.

Jones, J. (2008). Patterns of revision in on-line writing: A study of Wikipedia's featured articles. *Written Communication* **25**(2): 262–289.

Keren, M. (2006). *Blogosphere: The New Political Arena.* Lanham, MD, Lexington Books.

Kline, D. and D. Burstein (2005). *Blog! How the Newest Media Revolution is Changing Politics, Business, and Culture.* New York, CDS Books.

Kluth, A. (2006). Among the audience: A survey of New Media. *The Economist.* 22 April.

Kumar, R., J. Novak, P. Raghavan and A. Tomkins (2004). Structure and Evolution of Blogspace. *Communications of the ACM* **47**(12): 35–39.

Lanham, R. (1968). *A Handlist of Rhetorical Terms.* Berkeley, CA, University of California Press.

Lanier, J. (2006). Digital Maoism: The hazards of the new online collectivism. *The Edge.* http://www.edge.org/3rd_culture/lanier06/lanier06_index.html

Lankshear, C. and M. Knobel (2006). *New Literacies: Everyday Practices and Classroom Learning.* Milton Keynes, Open University Press.

Leech, G. (1983). *Principles of Pragmatics.* Harlow, Longman.

Levinson, S. (1983). *Pragmatics.* Cambridge, Cambridge University Press.

Marlow, C. (2004). Audience, structure and authority in the weblog community. International Communication Association, New Orleans. http://alumni.media.mit.edu/~cameron/cv/pubs/04-01.html

—(2006). Linking without thinking: Weblogs, readership and online social capital formation. International Communication Association Conference, Dresden, Germany. http://alumni.media.mit.edu/~cameron/cv/pubs/2006-linking-without-thinking

Massey, D. (1994). *Space, Place, and Gender.* Cambridge, Polity.

McHenry, R. (2004). The Faith-based Encyclopedia. *TCSDaily: Technology, Commerce, Society.* http://www.tcsdaily.com/article.aspx?id=111504A

McQuail, D. (1997). *Audience Analysis.* London, Sage.

Meyrowitz, J. (1985). *No Sense of Place: The Impact of Electronic Media on Social Behavior.* New York, Oxford University Press.

Miller, C. and D. Shepherd (2004). Blogging as social action: A genre analysis of the weblog. *Into the Blogosphere: Rhetoric, Community, and Culture of Weblogs.* L. J. Gurak, S. Antonijevic, L. Johnson, C. Ratliff and J. Reyman. http://blog.lib.umn.edu/blogosphere/blogging_as_social_action_a_genre_analysis_of_the_weblog.html

Miller, D. and D. Slater (2000). *The Internet: An Ethnographic Approach.* Oxford, Berg.

Mühlhäusler, P. and R. Harré (1990). *Pronouns and People.* Oxford, Blackwell.

174

Myers, G. (2006). 'Where are you from?' Identifying place. *Journal of Sociolinguistics* **10**(3): 316–339.

Nilsson, S. (2004). A brief overview of linguistic aspects of the blogosphere, English Department, Umeå University.

Nowson, S. (2006). The Language of weblogs: A Study of genre and individual differences. School of Informatics. Edinburgh, University of Edinburgh. http://www.era.lib.ed.ac.uk/handle/1842/1113

O'Reilly, T. (2005). *What is Web 2.0.* http://www.oreillynet.com/pub/a/oreilly/tim/news/2005/09/30/what-is-web-20.html

Palmer, F. (1990). *Modality and the English Modals.* London, Longman.

Paltridge, B. (1997). *Genre, Frames and Writing in Research Settings.* Amsterdam, John Benjamins.

Pfeil, U., P. Zaphiris and C. S. Ang (2006). Cultural differences in collaborative authoring of Wikipedia. *Journal of Computer-Mediated Communication* **12**(1). http://jcmc.indiana.edu/vol12/issue1/pfeil.html

Polanyi, L. (1985). *Telling the American Story : A Cultural and Structural analysis of Conversational Storytelling.* Norwood, New Jersey, Ablex.

Posteguillo, S. (2003). *Netlinguistics: An Analytical Framework to Study Language, Discourse and Ideology in Internet.* Castelló de la Plana, Publicacions de la Universitat Jaume I.

Priedhorsky, R., J. Chen, S. Lam, K. Panciera, L. Turveen and J. Riedl (2007). Creating, destroying, and restoring value in Wikipedia. Group '07, Sanibel Island, Florida. http://www-users.cs.umn.edu/~reid/papers/group282-priedhorsky.pdf

Project for Excellence in Journalism (2006). The State of the News Media.

Renkema, J. (2004). *Introduction to Discourse Studies.* Amsterdam, John Benjamins.

Rodzvilla, J., Ed. (2002). *We've Got Blog: How Weblogs are Changing Our Culture.* Cambridge, MA, Perseus Books.

Rosenzweig, R. (2006). Can History Be Open Source? *Wikipedia* and the Future of the Past. *The Journal of American History*: 117–146.

Schegloff, E. (1972). Notes on a conversational practice: Formulating place. *Studies in Social Interaction.* D. Sudnow. New York, Free Press: 75–119.

Schrøder, K., K. Drontner, S. Kline and C. Murray (2003). *Researching Audiences.* London, Arnold.

Scollon, R. and S. W. Scollon (2003). *Discourses in Place: Language in the Material World.* London, Routledge.

Semino, E. and M. Short (2004). *Corpus Stylistic: Speech, Writing and Thought Presentation in a Corpus of English Writing.* London, Routledge.

Shirky, C. (2008). *Here Comes Everybody: The Power of Organizing without Organizations.* London, Allen Lane.

Singer, J. B. (2006). Journalists and news bloggers: Complements, contradictions, and challenges. *The Uses of Blogs.* A. Bruns and J. Jacobs. New York, Peter Lang: 23–32.

Stone, B. (2004). *Who Let the Blogs Out?: A Hyperconnected Peek a the World of Weblogs.* New York, St. Martins.

Stubbs, M. (1996). *Text and Corpus Analysis : Computer Assisted Studies of Language and Institutions*. Cambridge, MA, Blackwell Publishers.

Swales, J. (1990). *Genre Analysis*. Cambridge, Cambridge University Press.

Thelwall, M. (2003). What is this link doing here? Beginning a fine-grained process of identifying reasons for academic hyperlink creation. *Information Research* **8**(3): 151.

Thompson, G. and P. Thetela (1995). The sound of one hand clapping: The management of interaction in written discourse. *Text* **15**(1): 103–127.

Thrift, N. (1997). 'Us' and 'Them': Re-imagining places, re-imagining identities. *Consumption and Everyday Life*. H. Mackay. London, Sage: 159–212.

Tosca, S. P. (2000). A Pragmatics of Links. *Journal of Digital Information* **1**(6): Article No. 22, 27-06-2000-.

Viégas, F., M. Wattenberg, and K. Dave (2004). Studying cooperation and conflict between authors with history flow visualisations. CHI 2004. http://alumni.media.mit.edu/~fviegas/papers/history_flow.pdf

Viégas, F., M. Wattenberg, J. Kriss and F. van Ham (2007). Talk before you type: coordination in Wikipedia. 40th Annual Hawai'i International Conference on System Sciences. http://www.research.ibm.com/visual/papers/wikipedia_coordination_final.pdf

Warner, M. (2002). Publics and counterpublics. *Public Culture* **14**(1): 49–90.

Watts, R. (2003). *Politeness*. Cambridge, Cambridge University Press.

Wenger, E. (1998). *Communities of Practice: Learning, Meaning, and Identity*. Cambridge, Cambridge University Press.

Wilson, J. (1990). *Politically Speaking: The Pragmatic Analysis of Political Language*. Oxford, Blackwell.

Wodak, R. (2001). The discourse-historical approach. *Methods of Critical Discourse Analysis*. R. Wodak and M. Meyer. London, Sage: 63–94.

Zelizer, B. (2004). *Taking Journalism Seriously: News and the Academy*. Thousand Oaks, Sage.

Index